Wonderlic®

Basic Skills Test Practice Questions

DEAR FUTURE EXAM SUCCESS STORY

First of all, **THANK YOU** for purchasing Mometrix study materials!

Second, congratulations! You are one of the few determined test-takers who are committed to doing whatever it takes to excel on your exam. **You have come to the right place.** We developed these practice tests with one goal in mind: to deliver you the best possible approximation of the questions you will see on test day.

Standardized testing is one of the biggest obstacles on your road to success, which only increases the importance of doing well in the high-pressure, high-stakes environment of test day. Your results on this test could have a significant impact on your future, and these practice tests will give you the repetitions you need to build your familiarity and confidence with the test content and format to help you achieve your full potential on test day.

Your success is our success

We would love to hear from you! If you would like to share the story of your exam success or if you have any questions or comments in regard to our products, please contact us at **800-673-8175** or **support@mometrix.com**.

Thanks again for your business and we wish you continued success!

Sincerely,
The Mometrix Test Preparation Team

Written and edited by the Mometrix Exam Secrets Test Prep Team
Printed in the United States of America

Table of Contents

Practice Test #1

Verbal

1. For locating information in a library card catalog, which of these is included within the bibliographic description of an item?

A. Subject headings
B. The call number
C. Title and edition
D. Added entries

2. In today's libraries, which of these formats for materials are shelved together?

A. Books and journals
B. Books and databases
C. Books and multimedia
D. None of these formats

3. Which of the following library tools should a user consult to find articles on specific subjects within periodicals?

A. An index
B. Card catalog
C. A microfiche
D. Any/all of these

4. The subject content textbooks that you were given or assigned to use in school are typically examples of which type of information source?

A. Primary sources
B. Secondary sources
C. Tertiary sources only
D. Any of these equally

5. How-to directions contain higher proportions of which type(s) of words and their concepts?

A. Negatives, adjectives, prepositions, and conjunctions
B. Prepositions and conjunctions
C. Negatives and adjectives
D. Negatives only

6. Which of the following is an example of directions at the complex level?

A. "Please don't touch the biggest machine, or the one that is blue."
B. "Please clear all papers off of your desk and file them in drawers."
C. "Please throw your team's trash away before starting this project."
D. "Please deactivate all cell phones after you have taken your seats."

7. Among these, what is the best way both to test and to practice skills for following expanded and complex directions?

A. An activity involving correctly applying directions given in a verbal format
B. An activity involving correctly applying directions given in a visual format
C. An activity involving correctly matching verbal directions to visual images
D. An activity involving correctly writing and giving oral directions to others

8. In a quiz and/or practice activity, pictures of arrows point in different directions, each accompanied by one or more fractional numbers in different locations relative to the arrows; and questions like, "Which fraction is above the arrow that points to the right?" and "Which fraction is near the arrow that points to the left?" What do you have to observe and understand to answer these?

A. The directional terms used, "right" and "left"
B. Preposition meanings plus directional terms
C. The meanings of prepositions "above," "near"
D. Visual-spatial meanings of the pictures only

9. In Edgar Allan Poe's poem "The Bells," which of the following word pairs demonstrates the type of alliteration known as assonance?

A. "Molten-golden"
B. "Human heart"
C. "Runic rhyme"
D. "Brazen bells"

10. When reading an academic textbook, if you encounter an unfamiliar technical term or vocabulary word, which text feature within the same textbook can you use to find its definition?

A. An illustration
B. A dictionary
C. A glossary
D. A sidebar

11. Among the following author purposes for writing literature, which is likely to require the most interpretation on the part of the reader?

A. To inform
B. To entertain
C. To evoke moods
D. To satirize something

12. A history book that describes in detail all of the events leading up to a world war, showing how certain events precipitated others, uses which type of text structure?

A. Description
B. Problem-solution
C. Compare-contrast
D. Cause-and-effect

13. "Have you _______ the project yet?" Which choice is correct in this sentence context?

A. complete
B. completed
C. completing
D. completes

14. "When I was rereading the text, I notice several mistakes; maybe they will be corrected in the next edition." Where is there an error in this sentence?

A. "When I was rereading the text"
B. "I notice several mistakes"
C. "they will be corrected"
D. There is no error

15. "Following her makeover, Gloria was _______ to see her reflection in the mirror." Which word completes this sentence correctly for its context?

A. Transformed
B. Translated
C. Transfixed
D. Transferred

16. "The author's keen insights show how _______ she is." By context, which word correctly fills in the blank in this sentence?

A. Perspicacious
B. Perceptive
C. Oblivious
D. (a) or (b)

17. "Linda got hired by _______ her skills and experience." Which choice is *most* correct?

A. equivocating
B. vituperating
C. dissembling
D. impugning

18. The dodo bird is _______. Which word has the right meaning for this sentence?

A. Extra
B. Extant
C. Extinct
D. Extent

19. Someone who gains leadership by lying, distorting facts, and/or appealing to mass prejudices may be called which of these?

A. A demagogue
B. A pedagogue
C. A hemagogue
D. A synagogue

20. Which of the following has the meaning of menacing or threatening?

A. Minimum
B. Minatory
C. Minuscule
D. Minority

21. "John and Marcia had such a bad row the other evening that they are still hardly speaking." From the sentence context, which meaning of the underlined word is most appropriate?

A. A boat trip
B. A linear set
C. An argument
D. Any of these

22. "Whoopi often remarks that she hates to fly." Among multiple meanings, which is the meaning of the underlined word in this sentence context?

A. Operate or ride in an aircraft
B. Glide through the air on wings
C. A front opening in a pair of pants
D. Slang for fashionable or attractive

23. In which of the following sentences should the missing word be spelled *site*?

A. The joy on their faces was a beautiful ______.
B. He has set his ______s on the position of CEO.
C. ______-seeing is a popular activity on vacation.
D. The builders will be on the ______ next week.

24. The word *run* has different meanings in each of these sentences. In which one is it also used as a noun?

A. The musical *Cats* had an extraordinarily long run on Broadway.
B. She told them that she is determined to run her own business.
C. Every single time I try to run that software program, it crashes.
D. The buses run less frequently on weekends than on weekdays.

25. "There is nothing showy or clever, nothing cheap or meretricious in all their work." (Arthur Hayden, *Chats on Royal Copenhagen Porcelain*, 1918) Readers unfamiliar with the underlined word can determine which meaning from this sentence?

A. Flashy, showy, gaudy, or tawdry
B. False, deceptive, sham, insincere
C. Related to or typical of prostitutes
D. The meaning cannot be discerned

26. Spelling knowledge can help readers unfamiliar with the word mettlesome. Which of these is its correct meaning?

A. Bothersome/interferes
B. Made of a lot of metal
C. Courageous or spirited
D. Prying, nosy, intrusive

27. Which of the following does the word *quintessence* NOT mean?

A. The purest concentrated essence
B. The five most essential elements
C. The fifth essence or fifth element
D. The most perfect embodiment of

28. "Jack White and friends named their band The Raconteurs, suggesting that they relate tales by singing their songs." The meaning of *raconteur* can be determined from the sentence context as which of these?

A. Travelers
B. Musicians
C. Dealmakers
D. Storytellers

29. Which of the following is a complete sentence?

A. Raining all day and night.
B. While it was raining.
C. It was raining.
D. The rain.

30. What is correct regarding the following: "Sarah, who was the assistant to the executive."

A. This needs a predicate to be a complete sentence.
B. This requires a subject to be a complete sentence.
C. This needs no changes to be a complete sentence.
D. This must have a noun to be a complete sentence.

31. Which of the following sentences is/are complete as written?

A. Since they moved from the city to the country.
B. Since they moved from the city to the country, they are happier.
C. They moved from the city to the country.
D. (b) and (c) are both complete sentences, but (a) is not complete.

32. Among these, which choice is correctly written?

A. Bring your umbrella just in case.
B. Bring your umbrella it rains.
C. Bring your umbrella in case.
D. Bring your umbrella in case it rains.

33. Of the following, which version is BOTH a grammatically complete sentence AND ALSO does not change the meaning?

A. I always buy this food because my pets love it.
B. I always buy this food my pets love it.
C. Because my pets love it.
D. I always buy this food and my pets love it.

34. "Culinary experiences and activities are a burgeoning industry for the area as well as the state and is bringing in more revenue from tourism than ever." What is wrong with this sentence?

A. It contains a dangling participle.
B. It lacks subject-verb agreement.
C. It includes several split infinitives.
D. It has nothing wrong; it is correct.

35. "A new series of classes is beginning at the college." Which is the correct form?

A. A new series of classes are beginning at the college.
B. A new series of classes will beginning at the college.
C. The sentence is already correct as it is written above.
D. A new series of class is now beginning at the college.

36. "The majority of the people agree." What is correct grammatically?

A. The sentence is correct as written.
B. The majority of the people agrees.
C. Either (a) or (b) can be acceptable.
D. Neither (a) nor (b) is grammatical.

37. "The president, as well as the joint chiefs of staff, are on the way." Which choice is the correct one?

A. This sentence is already grammatically correct as written above.
B. The president, and also the joint chiefs of staff, is on the way.
C. The president and the joint chiefs of staff is on the way.
D. The president, as well as the joint chiefs of staff, is on the way.

38. "We advise that every new employee ______ the questionnaire as soon as possible." Which correctly fills in the blank?

A. should complete
B. complete
C. completes
D. completed

39. "If we finish this on time, our manager will ______ an extra break." What is the correct phrase to complete this with standard sentence structure?

A. let us to take
B. let us take
C. allow us take
D. allow that we take

40. "When you look at the map, you can see ______ to the east of the city." Standard syntax would fill the blank with which of the following?

A. that our suburb placed
B. our suburb there is
C. that our suburb lies
D. our suburb laying

41. A complete and correct sentence with standard structure is which one of these?

A. The feeling of warm sand between the toes.
B. Feeling warm sand in between your toes.
C. I like feeling warm sand between my toes.
D. I like feeling warm sand run through toes.

42. Of the following versions, which is a standard sentence?

A. Watching themselves making footprints in the mud.
B. The children watching themselves making footprints.
C. The children are watch themselves making footprints.
D. The children are watching themselves make footprints.

43. Although many constituents agree with him, ________. Which choice correctly completes this sentence?

A. few will actually vote for his bill.
B. and so they will vote for his bill.
C. they are likely to vote for his bill.
D. they are going to vote for his bill.

44. In Clement Moore's famed poem "A Visit from St. Nicholas" (1823) [better known by opening line "'Twas the night before Christmas...."] is this verse: "He was chubby and plump, a right jolly old elf, / And I laughed when I saw him in spite of myself." What type of sentence is this?

A. A simple sentence
B. A complex sentence
C. A compound sentence
D. A compound-complex sentence

45. "After supper, I am going to the choir rehearsal in the basement of the old school building across the street from the grocery store, and then food shopping." What is this sentence structure?

A. Complex
B. Compound
C. Compound-complex
D. It is a simple sentence

46. "His talent made him famous; however, he was painfully shy, reclusive, and suffered from crippling stage fright." What kind of structure does this sentence have?

A. It is a compound sentence.
B. This is compound-complex.
C. This is a complex sentence.
D. It is just a simple sentence.

47. Which choice corrects errors in this compound sentence? "She liked him; nevertheless, she refused to go out with him."

A. She liked him, nevertheless; she refused to go out with him.
B. She liked him, nevertheless, she refused to go out with him.
C. This compound sentence is correct as in the question above.
D. She liked him, nevertheless she refused to go out with him.

48. "I got so many things accomplished, you were sleeping." Which choice will correct this sentence AND give it a complex sentence structure?

A. I got so many things accomplished, and you were sleeping.
B. I got things done and I took a walk while you were sleeping.
C. I got so many things accomplished while you were sleeping.
D. I got so many things done and walked during your sleeping.

49. Which of these is a compound sentence without errors?

A. It was raining hard all that evening so she did not take out the garbage.
B. It was raining hard all that evening; so she did not take out the garbage.
C. It was raining hard all that evening and she did not take out the garbage.
D. It was raining hard all that evening, so she did not take out the garbage.

50. Of the following, which version has compound-complex sentence structure and is also free of any grammatical or mechanical errors?

A. Tom always showers before getting dressed, even after oversleeping, and then goes to work.
B. Tom always showers before he gets dressed, even if he oversleeps, and then he goes to work.
C. Tom always showers before he gets dressed even after oversleeping; and then he goes to work.
D. Tom always showers before getting dressed even after oversleeping, and then going on to work.

Mathematics

1. Which line graph correctly reflects the data shown in the table?

Time	Number of Customers
2:00 p.m.	20
4:00 p.m.	30
6:00 p.m.	50
8:00 p.m.	10

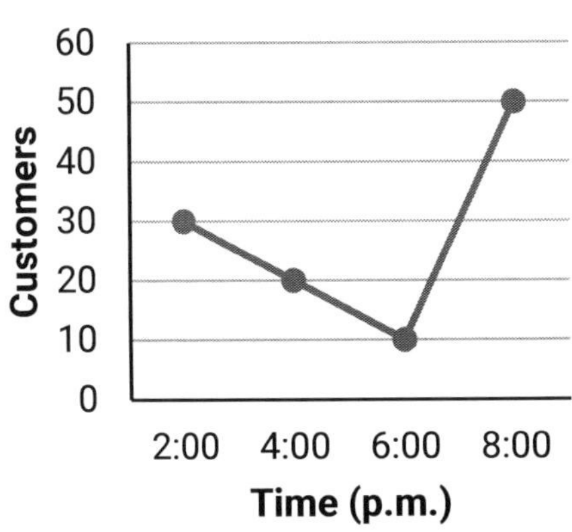

A.

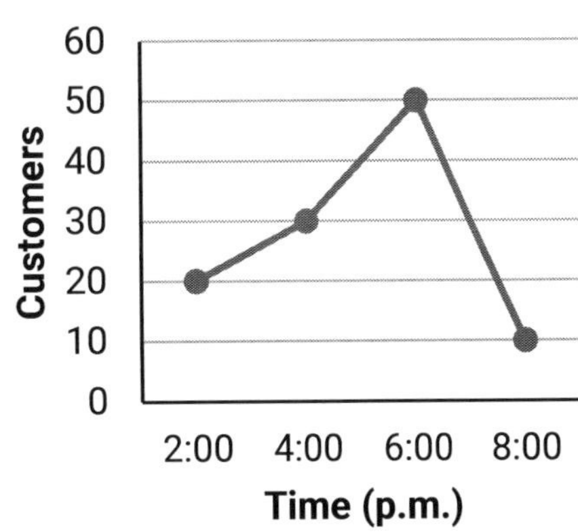

B.

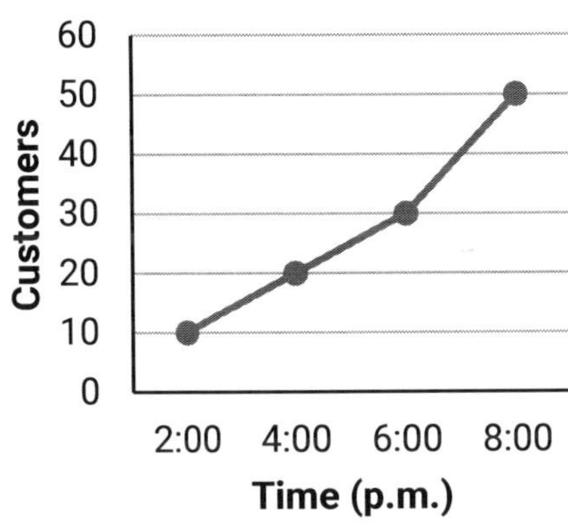

C.

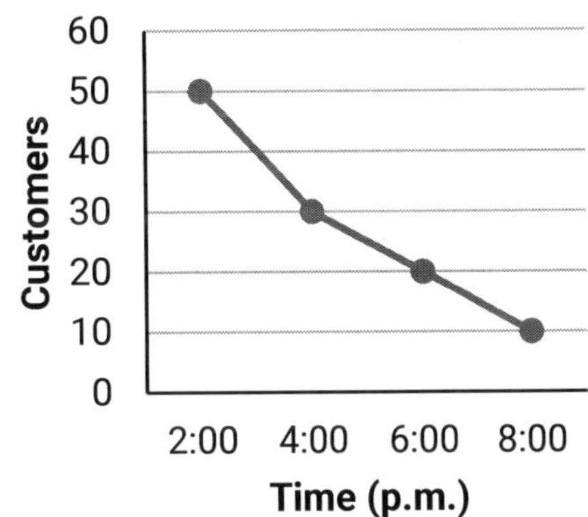

D.

2. The number of gallons of water emptying out of a pool each minute is given in the following table.

Minute	1	2	3	4
Gallons	28	19	12	7

How many gallons of water should be expected to empty out of the pool on the fifth minute?

A. 3
B. 4
C. 5
D. 9

3. The length of the football field near Gerald's school is 120 yards. What is the length of the field in feet?

A. 1,440 feet
B. 400 feet
C. 360 feet
D. 12 feet

4. A recipe calls for $3\frac{3}{4}$ cups of flour. Which fraction below is equivalent to this amount?

A. $\frac{5}{2}$
B. $\frac{15}{4}$
C. $\frac{3}{2}$
D. $\frac{9}{4}$

5. A large rectangular-prism-shaped tank at the zoo is 8 feet wide and 5 feet high. How long is the tank if it holds a volume of 200 cubic feet of water?

A. 5 feet
B. 6 feet
C. 8 feet
D. 13 feet

6. A rectangular plot in a garden is 3 times longer than it is wide. What is the perimeter of the garden if it has a width of 8 meters?

A. 24 meters
B. 23 meters
C. 64 meters
D. 192 meters

7. A length of string is measured to be $\frac{31}{8}$ inches. Between which two points on the ruler below will this length lie?

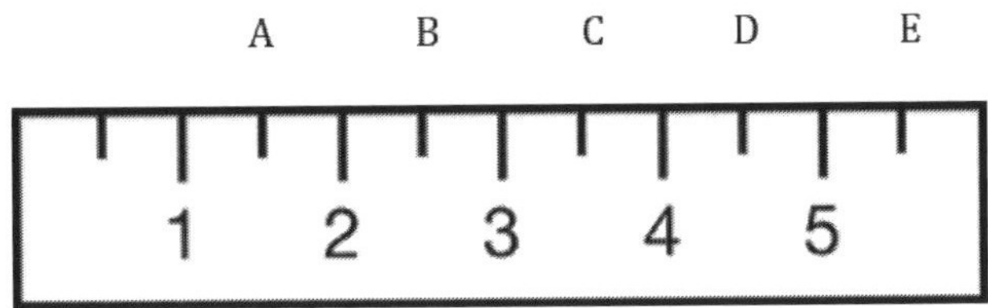

A. Between points A and B
B. Between points B and C
C. Between points C and D
D. Between points D and E

8. The number of customers in a new restaurant is given in the table below.

Week	Customers
1	155
2	180
3	205

How many customers should be expected in week 4?

A. 200
B. 225
C. 230
D. 255

9. Mr. Thompson fills his 25.2 gallon gasoline tank with gas that costs $2.98 a gallon. Which is the best approximation of the cost of the gasoline?

A. $50
B. $60
C. $75
D. $90

10. Glenda poured salt into three salt shakers from a box that contained 26 ounces of salt. She poured 2 ounces of salt into one shaker, 3 ounces of salt into the second shaker, and 4 ounces into the third shaker. She did not pour salt into any other shakers. Which expression best represents the amount of salt left in the box after Glenda poured salt into the three shakers?

A. $2 - 3 - 4 + 26$
B. $2 + 3 + 4 - 26$
C. $26 - 2 + 3 + 4$
D. $26 - 2 - 3 - 4$

11. A bookshelf is to be $7\frac{5}{8}$ inches wide. Which of the following fractions is equivalent to this measurement?

A. $\frac{35}{8}$
B. $\frac{75}{8}$
C. $\frac{61}{8}$
D. $\frac{43}{8}$

12. One morning at Jim's café, 25 people ordered juice, 10 ordered milk, and 50 ordered coffee with breakfast. Which ratio best compares the number of people who ordered milk to the number of people who ordered juice?

A. 5 to 7
B. 5 to 2
C. 2 to 7
D. 2 to 5

13. A man earns $15.23 per hour and gets a raise of $2.34 per hour. What is his new hourly rate of pay?

A. $12.89
B. $15.46
C. $17.57
D. $35.64

14. Jodi made a sum of money yesterday at a bake sale. She spent half of the money to buy more ingredients for next week's bake sale and then spent $12 to go to the movies. Jodi has $17 remaining. How much did she make yesterday at the bake sale?

A. $36
B. $41
C. $46
D. $58

15. If $2x = 5x - 30$, what is the value of x?

A. -10
B. -4.3
C. 4.3
D. 10

16. Which of the following is correct?

A. $\frac{4}{7} = \frac{12}{21}$
B. $\frac{3}{4} = \frac{12}{20}$
C. $\frac{5}{8} = \frac{15}{32}$
D. $\frac{7}{9} = \frac{28}{45}$

17. William is going to work out of the country for a total of 145 days. How long will William be gone expressed in weeks and days?

A. 20 weeks and 5 days
B. 21 weeks and 2 days
C. 24 weeks and 1 day
D. 29 weeks

18. In ice hockey, the number of points a player scores is defined as the sum of the number of goals and the number of assists. Which hockey player listed in the table below has the highest number of points?

Player	Goals	Assists
Phillips	2	23
Jackson	5	17
Robinson	13	15
Miller	8	19

A. Phillips
B. Jackson
C. Robinson
D. Miller

19. The side length of a regular pentagon is 6.5 centimeters. What is the perimeter of this figure?

A. 26.0 cm
B. 32.5 cm
C. 39.0 cm
D. 42.25 cm

20. A little boy decides to give away all his marbles. Each of his 4 friends is to receive an equal share. Which of the statements below describes how this can be done?

A. Multiply his marbles by 4 and give this amount to each of his friends.
B. Multiply his marbles by 2 and give this amount to each of his friends.
C. Multiply his marbles by $\frac{1}{2}$ and give this amount to each of his friends.
D. Multiply his marbles by $\frac{1}{4}$ and give this amount to each of his friends.

21. The number of members in a ski club is shown in the table below.

Year	Members
2008	19
2009	31
2010	43

How many ski club members would be expected for 2011?

A. 50
B. 55
C. 62
D. 78

22. Two sisters were arguing over who could have a larger piece of pie. Their mother told the older daughter she could have $\frac{2}{5}$ of the pie. She told the younger daughter she could have $\frac{1}{3}$ of the pie. Which daughter received a larger piece of pie?

A. The older daughter received the larger piece.
B. The younger daughter received the larger piece.
C. Both pieces are the same size.
D. There is not enough information to determine which piece is larger.

23. If $\frac{x}{3} + 7 = 35$, what is the value of x?

A. 9.33
B. 14
C. 84
D. 126

24. In the United States, 95% of all men are between 5 feet 3 inches and 6 feet 2 inches tall. Which measurement below is outside of this range?

A. 5′1"
B. 5′7"
C. 5′11"
D. 6′1"

25. Enrique used a formula to find the total cost, in dollars, for repairs he and his helper, Jenny, made to a furnace. The expression below shows the formula he used, with 4 being the number of hours he worked on the furnace and 2 being the number of hours Jenny worked on the furnace.

$$20 + 35(4 + 2) + 47$$

What is the total cost for repairing the furnace?

A. $189
B. $269
C. $277
D. $377

26. What is the volume of a rectangular prism with a height of 10 cm, a length of 5 cm, and a width of 6 cm?

A. 30 cm^3
B. 60 cm^3
C. 150 cm^3
D. 300 cm^3

27. The total number of students that passed their swimming test is shown in the table below.

Week	1	2	3	4
Number passed	16	25	32	37

How many students are predicted to have passed by week 5?

A. 46
B. 44
C. 40
D. 39

28. Matthew wants to buy a video game that costs $25. He only has $18. How much additional money does Matthew need to save to purchase the game?

A. $5
B. $6
C. $7
D. $8

29. An average apple weighs 150 grams. What would be the approximate weight of a dozen apples?

A. 0.9 kilograms
B. 1.2 kilograms
C. 1.5 kilograms
D. 1.8 kilograms

30. Harold learned that 6 out of 10 students at his school live within two miles of the school. If 240 students attend Grade 6 at his school, about how many of these students should Harold expect to live within two miles of the school?

A. 24
B. 40
C. 144
D. 180

31. Gillian is deciding between two data plans for her cellphone. Plan A provides 2.5 GB of data for a flat rate of $20/month and charges $15 per GB for any extra use. Plan B provides unlimited data for $50/month. What amount of data would Gillian have to use in a month for both plans to cost the same amount?

A. 2 GB
B. 3.5 GB
C. 3.75 GB
D. 4.5 GB

32. Large boxes of canned beans hold 24 cans of beans and small boxes hold 12 cans. One afternoon, Gerald brought 4 large boxes of canned beans and 6 small boxes of canned beans to the food bank. How many cans of beans did Gerald bring to the food bank that afternoon?

A. 168
B. 192
C. 288
D. 360

33. Mr. Foster wants to put new carpet on the floor of his rectangular playroom. The playroom is 27 feet long and 18 feet wide. He has found an inexpensive carpet that is priced $14 per square yard. What would be a reasonable price for enough carpet to cover the floor of his playroom?

A. $486
B. $756
C. $1,260
D. $2,268

34. Phil is going to school overseas for 9 weeks and 5 days. How many days will Phil be gone?

A. 44
B. 59
C. 68
D. 95

35. Which of the following is correct?

A. $\frac{2}{3} = \frac{18}{24}$
B. $\frac{4}{5} = \frac{16}{20}$
C. $\frac{1}{9} = \frac{4}{18}$
D. $\frac{3}{8} = \frac{9}{16}$

36. Elena counted the number of birds that came to her bird bath one afternoon. While she watched, 20 sparrows, 16 finches, 4 wrens, and 10 jays came to the bird bath. Which ratio, in simplest form, compares the number of finches that Elena counted to the number of sparrows?

A. 4 : 5
B. 4 : 9
C. 16 : 20
D. 20 : 36

37. The recipe Mary is using to bake cupcakes requires 1 cup of milk and makes 8 cupcakes. If she needs to make 32 cupcakes for the party, how much milk is needed?

A. 1 pint
B. 1 gallon
C. 3 cups
D. 1 quart

38. A survey of a random sample of 100 drivers asked them the color of their car. The results of the survey are presented in the table below.

Color of car	Number of drivers
Blue	26
Red	14
Yellow	36
Silver	24

If the parking lot at the local store is filled with 25 cars, how many yellow cars would be expected to be in the lot?

A. 6
B. 9
C. 11
D. 12

39. Mr. Aguilera needs 71 feet of fencing that costs $3.98 per foot. Which of the following is the best approximation for the price of the fencing?

A. $210
B. $240
C. $280
D. $320

40. A square flower garden has an area of 81 feet. What is the length of one side of the garden?

A. 9 feet
B. 20.25 feet
C. 40.5 feet
D. 324 feet

41. The tires on Ginny's bike are about 20 inches from the top of the tire to the ground. Which of these is closest to the distance around each tire?

A. 60 inches
B. 180 inches
C. 400 inches
D. 1,200 inches

42. In the figure below, line segments $\overline{AB}$ and $\overline{CD}$ are parallel and are intersected by a third line. If $\alpha = 135°$, what is the measure of δ?

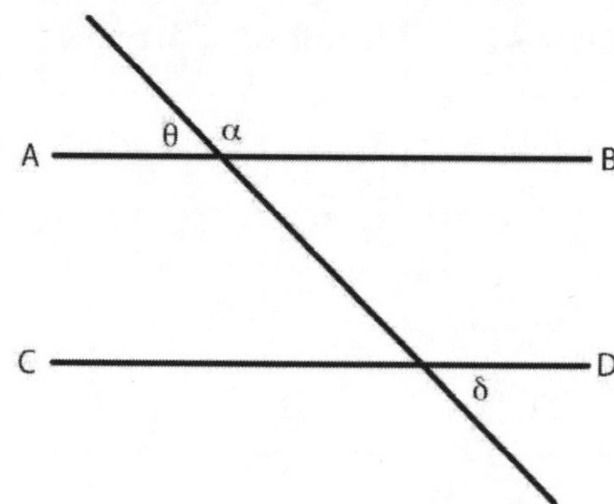

A. 135°
B. 45°
C. 35°
D. 30°

43. Which line graph correctly reflects the data shown in the table?

Month	Number of Carnivals
February	2
June	8
August	5
October	10

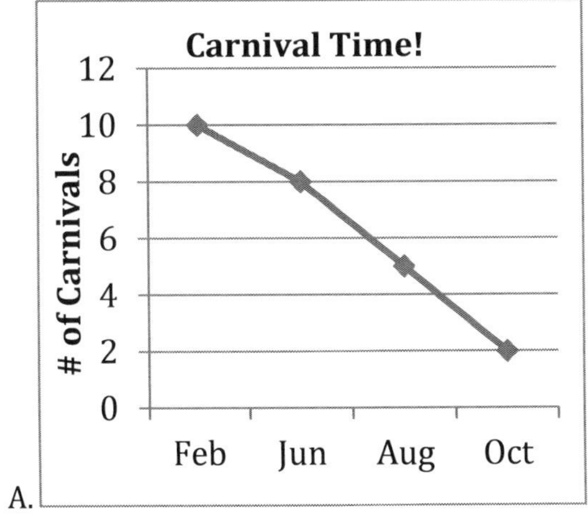

A.

B.
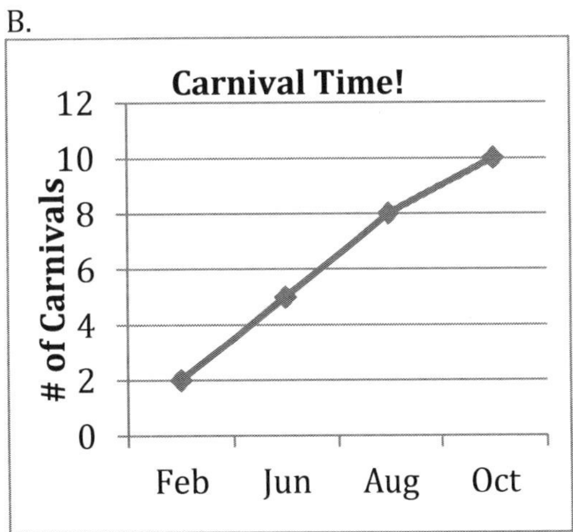

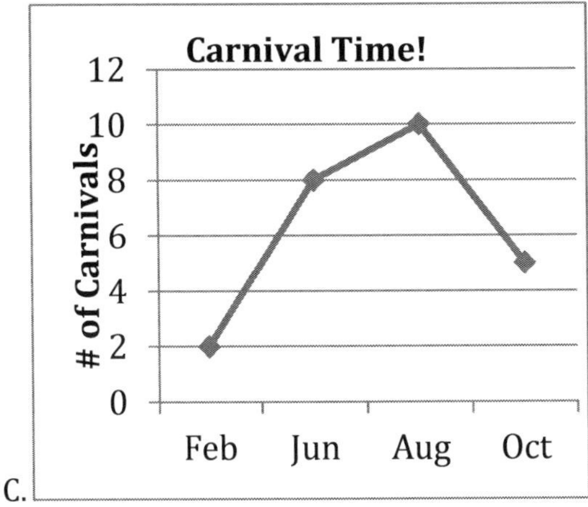

C.

D.
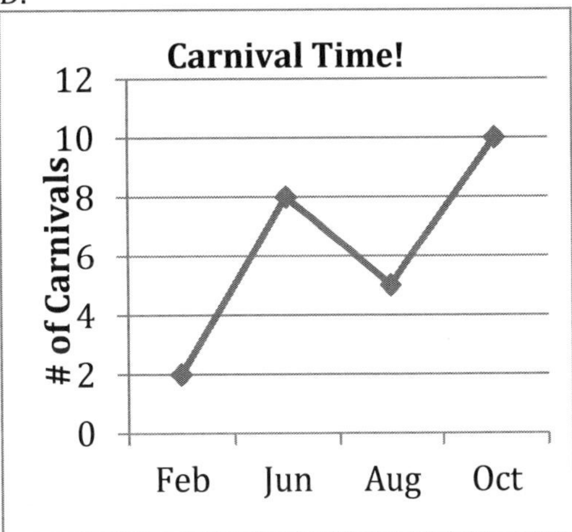

44. Four students were given a typing test measuring their speed in words per minute and then given the same typing test several weeks later. Which student had the greatest improvement?

Student	**First Score (words per minute)**	**Second Score (words per minute)**
Alexander	22	39
Betty	39	48
Carolyn	27	43
David	22	42

A. Alexander
B. Betty
C. Carolyn
D. David

45. $\angle AEC$ **is a straight angle.** $m\angle BEC$ **is 45°. What is** $m\angle AEB$**?**

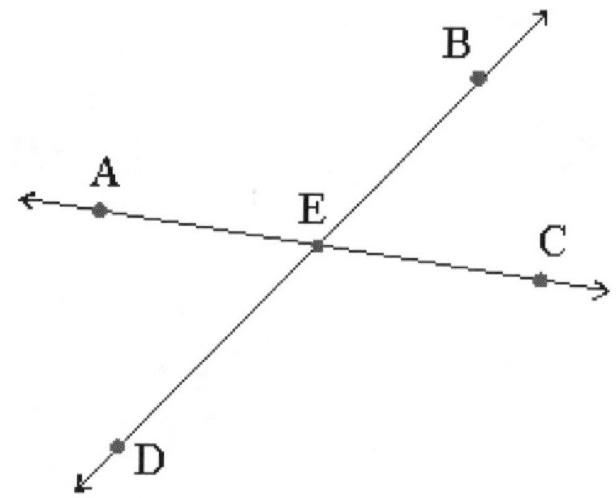

A. 90°
B. 115°
C. 135°
D. 180°

Answer Key and Explanations for Test #1

Verbal

1. C: Included in a paper or electronic library card catalog are the main entry, additional entries (d), subject headings (a), the call number (b) of the item (also called the classification number), and a bibliographic description of the item. Within that description is included the item's title, edition (c), publication information, physical description, statement of responsibility, material-specific details, standard numbers, the series the item is part of, and any notes.

2. D: In today's libraries, books are shelved in separate areas from journals (a), magazines, newspapers, electronic databases (b), microfilm or microfiche, materials recorded on CD-ROMs, and materials in multimedia (c) formats like audio and video recordings, slides, etc.

3. A: The index is a library tool that lists which issue and/or volume number of every periodical in the collection contains an article(s) on a specific subject, including dates and the article's page numbers. Users can look under the subject headings to find articles. The card catalog (b) is a library tool whereby users can identify and then physically locate *books* available in the collection. Microfiche (c) is a *format* in which periodicals, newspapers, and other collection items may be available rather than an actual tool for accessing those items. Since only (a) is correct, (d) is incorrect.

4. B: Subject content textbooks in math, social studies, history, sciences, English language arts, etc. are typically secondary sources. Primary sources (a) are used in school too; but they are original works, e.g. novels, books of poetry, books of short stories, plays, etc. for English language arts; or firsthand accounts like journals, diaries, letters, news reports or articles, etc. written during the time period studied for history, which you may have been assigned to read in school along with subject textbooks. You probably also used tertiary sources (c) in school, but as references—e.g. encyclopedias, bibliographies, abstracts, etc.

5. A: How-to directions contain higher proportions of negatives (d), e.g. do not, don't, is not, isn't, are not, aren't, etc., adjectives (c), e.g. even-numbered/odd-numbered; yellow, blue, red, other colors; underlined, boldfaced, italicized; bigger, smaller, same, different, round, square, etc., prepositions (b), e.g. above, below, with, inside, outside, around, behind, etc., and conjunctions (b), e.g. and, or, nor, since, because, as, therefore, both, etc. To follow directions correctly, readers must attend to these words and the concepts they communicate.

6. D: This is an example of complex directions because it is a complex sentence with an independent clause and a dependent clause, contains two steps, and uses syntax and vocabulary that develop later in language skills acquisition. Choice (a) is an example of expanded one-step directions, which include only one step but also contractions, negatives, and slightly more advanced vocabulary than basic one-step directions (e.g. "Please clear your desk."). Choice (b) is an example of basic two-step directions, which contain two steps, often as two independent clauses joined by a conjunction as they are here. Choice (c) is an example of expanded two-step directions, which add a structure to the two steps (in this case, the dependent clause introduced by "before").

7. C: Of these choices, the best way to evaluate and practice skills for following expanded and complex directions is an activity that requires matching verbal directions to choices of visual images. This shows whether an individual understands the language in the directions. Choice (a) restricts the activity to a verbal format, omitting another modality to demonstrate comprehension.

Choice (b) limits the format to visuals, preventing evaluating or practicing comprehension of verbal directions. Choice (d) requires individuals to write and orally give directions before learning, practicing, or being tested on understanding and following them, which come first.

8. B: To answer these types of questions correctly, you must not only understand the spatial directional concepts of left and right and notice which way each of the arrows is pointing, but also notice which prepositions are used in the questions and what they mean. Only knowing right and left (a) is not enough; neither is only knowing which way the arrows point in the pictures (d), or only knowing what "above," "near," (c), etc. mean.

9. A: Alliteration involves the repetition of sounds in words adjacent to or near each other. When consonant sounds (particularly word-initial ones) are repeated in two or more words, the alliteration is called consonance. Choices (b), (c), and (d) are all examples of consonance. When vowel sounds in words are repeated across words, this type of alliteration is called assonance. Choice (a) is an example of assonance.

10. C: A glossary defines the most important technical terms/vocabulary words used in the text. An illustration (a), in addition to visual interest, can inform many aspects of settings, scenes, characters, action, etc., but only illustrates some specific word/term meanings sometimes, not all the most important ones. A dictionary (b) is not a text feature within the same textbook; it is a separate reference. A sidebar (d), i.e. a text box sometimes including graphics at one side of a page, focuses in detail on a more specific aspect/example/issue within a subject.

11. D: When the purpose is to inform (a), readers know because most/all text provides facts, explains reasons, or gives procedural directions. Readers recognize entertainment (b) when amused by description/dialogue, excited by action, perplexed by mystery, or in such suspense to discover what happens they cannot put down the text. Readers recognize evoking moods (c) in word choices connoting sadness, fear, elation, etc. Satire (d) requires more interpretation; for example, in "A Modest Proposal," Jonathan Swift wrote in a "deadpan" tone, as if seriously suggesting cannibalism as an economic and social solution, to lampoon English society.

12. D: The question includes that the book shows how certain events precipitated others and led to a war; this is an example of cause-and-effect text structure, which explains or demonstrates which events or motivations produce which results, i.e. which causes produce which effects. Description (a) does not show cause-and-effect but paints a vivid picture for readers to feel they are experiencing directly. Problem-solution (b) structure presents a dilemma, issue, or mystery and then offers a solution. Comparison-contrast (c) identifies similarities and differences between/among things.

13. B: The sentence context shows by the auxiliary verb "have" that the verb's tense is present perfect, i.e. "completed." "Complete" (a) would be the present tense or part of the infinitive "to complete" (e.g. "Did you complete it?" where the auxiliary verb "to do" is past tense but "complete" is uninflected; or "Do you complete it?") and is thus incorrect. "Completing" (c) is the progressive (aka continuous) participle (e.g. "Are you completing it?"), hence also incorrect. "Completes" (d) is the third-person singular (e.g. "S/he completes it"); neither the second-person "you" nor the present perfect "have completed" takes the *–s* ending.

14. B: The error is that the verb "notice" is in the present tense, whereas the dependent clause "When I was rereading the text" (a) introducing the sentence is in the past tense. Therefore, "notice" should be "notice**d**" to be correct. The clause "they will be corrected" (c), introduced by the adverb "maybe," expresses a future possibility and is correctly written in the future tense. Since (b) has an error, (d) is incorrect.

15. C: The correct choice is "transfixed," i.e. rendered motionless, as with amazement or awe in this case (or with fear/terror in other cases). If the sentence read only, "Following her makeover, Gloria was _______," then "transformed" (a) would be correct, meaning the makeover had transformed or completely changed her appearance. However, seeing her reflection in the mirror would not change Gloria's appearance. "Translated" (b) means to convert, e.g. from Spanish to English or from intentions to actions. "Transferred" (d) means moved or passed from one place/person to another.

16. D: Perspicacious (a) and perceptive (b) are synonyms meaning astute, discerning, insightful, or intuitive. Either one fits the sentence context. Oblivious (c) means unaware and is a near antonym (opposite) of perceptive.

17. C: Dissembling means concealing, faking, or giving a misleading or false appearance to something. Equivocating (a) means speaking ambiguously about something. Linda would be more likely to get a job by misleading employers about her skills and appearance than by describing them ambiguously. Vituperating (b) means bitterly attacking something; Linda would not get the job by bitterly attacking her own skills and experience. Impugning (d) means challenging or questioning something; Linda would not get the job by challenging or questioning her own qualifications.

18. C: Extinct means no longer in existence, like the dodo bird. Extra (a) means more than what is needed or usual, or additional. Extant (b) means currently existing, i.e. the opposite or an antonym of extinct. Extent (d) means amount, degree, scope, length, distance, space, or volume.

19. A: A demagogue can mean simply a leader of the people, but more often has a cultural meaning of one who gains office/power by appealing to mass prejudices, often using lies and distortions. As a verb, it also means manipulating a political issue by distorting/obscuring it with prejudice, emotionalism, etc. A pedagogue (b) is a teacher. A hemagogue (c) is a substance that stimulates blood flow (used in medicine). A synagogue (d) is a Jewish temple. These words all have the same –*agogue* ending, meaning to lead. *Dem-* means people; *ped-* means children; *hem-* means blood; *syn-* means together.

20. B: Minatory (from Latin *minārī,* to threaten) means menacing or threatening. Minimum (a) means the least or smallest possible (from Latin *minimus*, smallest). Minuscule (c) means tiny/very small (from Latin *minus,* less, + *-cule,* a diminutive ending and variant of *–cle* as in *particle*). Minority (d) means the smaller number, amount, or part, i.e. less than half (from Latin *minor*, less/lesser/smaller or inferior/less important). Minimum, minuscule, and minority are all related to the same root meaning small/smaller/less; minatory has a different origin.

21. C: From the sentence context, an argument is the meaning of "row" here. Although it is possible that John and Marcia might still be hardly speaking after a bad boat trip (a), this is much less likely than after a bad argument. Having a bad linear set (b), e.g. a row of chairs in a room, of numbers on paper/screen, etc., does not make sense in this sentence and would be unlikely to cause such a rift. Since only (c) fits, (d) is incorrect.

22. A: *Fly* is a noun meaning a common insect; a verb meaning (a) or (b); a noun meaning (c); or a slang adjective meaning (d). Birds and insects, not humans, perform (b), ruling out this meaning. Pairing with "to" indicates "fly" is a verb infinitive, identifying part of speech and ruling out noun (c) and adjective (d) meanings. The subject named, a well-known celebrity (Whoopi Goldberg), often says she hates being an airplane passenger, further informing the meaning.

23. D: In sentences (a), (b), and (c), the missing word is spelled *sight*. In all three sentences, it is a noun; however, the meaning of each differs. In (a) it means something visible; in (b) it means aims for or aspires to (a figurative and idiomatic meaning); in (c) it means things worth seeing. In (d), the missing word is spelled *site*, a noun meaning a physical location.

24. A: In this sentence, *run* is used as a noun meaning the length of time that a play or show is performed or aired. In (b) it is used as a verb meaning to manage. In (c) it is used as a verb meaning to activate or use. In (d), it is used as a verb meaning to travel among places on a route and schedule.

25. A: If the word *meretricious* is unfamiliar to readers, they can determine its meaning in this sentence using context clues: the author also includes the adjectives "showy" and "cheap," which readers can assume from sentence structure are synonyms. Nothing in the sentence means or implies false, deceptive, sham, or insincere (b). The source title cited and the sentence itself are unrelated to prostitution (c). By process of elimination, (a) is the intended meaning among definitions for this word. Hence (d) is incorrect.

26. C: Readers unfamiliar with its meaning can rule out some meaning choices given here for *mettlesome* if they know correct spellings: Definition (a) is for *meddlesome,* an adjective describing someone or something as interfering or bothering someone. Someone who is prying, nosy, or intrusive (d) is another meaning for *meddlesome.* An adjective meaning made of/with metal (b) or like metal is *metallic.* After ruling out the other three, readers acquainted with the noun *mettle,* meaning courage, can also confirm the adjective derives from the noun: courageous is from courage as mettlesome is from mettle.

27. B: *Quintessence* derives from Medieval Latin *quīnta essentia,* meaning the fifth essence or fifth element (c). In ancient and medieval philosophies, the first four elements were earth, air, water, and fire; the fifth was ether, believed to be the matter of the heavenly bodies. This is its oldest meaning. Contemporary meanings today include (a) and (d). However, (b) is NOT a meaning.

28. D: The sentence context gives the clue "that they relate tales," informing the meaning of *raconteur* as someone who tells a story. This context clue is more reliable than hazarding guesses that from its sound, the word might mean travelers (a) or dealmakers (c); or simply assuming that because they are a band, it means musicians (c).

29. C: This is a complete sentence because it has a subject (it) and a verb (was raining). Choice (a) is not a sentence because it has no subject, only a verb and modifying adverbial phrase. Choice (b) is not a sentence because although it includes a subject and verb, it begins with the subordinating conjunction "while," making it a dependent clause requiring an independent clause to make a complete sentence. (Omitting "while" would make it an independent clause.) Choice (d) has only a subject/noun (rain) and article (the) with no verb.

30. A: This is not a complete sentence as it lacks a predicate; thus (c) is incorrect. Though "was" is a verb, it is part of the dependent clause, introduced by the relative pronoun "who" and modifying "Sarah." An example of this with a predicate added to make a complete sentence is, "Sarah, who was the assistant to the executive, greeted us." "Sarah" is the subject (b), and is also a noun (d)—a proper noun, i.e. a name.

31. D: (b) is a complete sentence that begins with a dependent clause and ends with an independent clause. (c) is a complete sentence consisting of one independent clause. However, (a) is not a complete sentence but a dependent clause with no independent clause to complete it. Dependent clauses cannot stand alone as sentences.

32. D: This is the only choice written correctly as a complete sentence. Choice (a) has the beginning of a dependent clause ("just in case") to modify the independent clause ("Bring your umbrella"), but it stops without finishing: just in case *what*? "It rains" is an independent clause/complete sentence by itself; "in case it rains" is a dependent clause introduced by "in case" and modifying "Bring your umbrella." Choice (b) is not a correct sentence; it may be considered a run-on for lacking punctuation to separate the two clauses. Choice (c) has the same error as (a).

33. A: This is a grammatically complete sentence, and its meaning includes an action (I always buy this food) and its reason (because my pets love it). Version (b) is a grammatically incorrect run-on sentence: Without a subordinating conjunction, it should be two sentences/clauses separated by a period/semicolon. Version (c) may sound right in spoken dialogue, but in writing is not a complete sentence, only a dependent clause without an independent clause. An alternative to adding an independent clause is removing "Because." Version (d) is a complete sentence BUT changes the meaning by changing "because" to "and," removing the reason.

34. B: This sentence lacks subject-verb agreement. The two subjects "experiences" and "activities" require the plural "are," which is the first (correct) verb; but the second ("bringing") has the singular "is", which does not agree. There is no dangling participle (a), which would leave a verb participle (like "bringing") without its subject. There are no split infinitives (c), which separate "to" and the rest of a verb's infinitive (e.g. "to really bring"). Since (b) is correct, (d) is incorrect. (Note: A comma is also needed between "state" and "and.")

35. C: This sentence is correct as written. The subject is "series," a singular noun; so the verb must also be singular ("is") to agree with the subject. Therefore, a plural subject ("are") as in (a) is incorrect. In (b), the present-tense auxiliary verb "is" is changed to the future "will," making no sense with the progressive participle "beginning." For future tense, "will *be*" is required for correct grammar; however, this would still change the meaning. In (d), making the object singular ("class") disagrees with "series," meaning multiple classes.

36. A: When the subject is a word indicating a portion, such as "majority," the rule for subject-verb agreement is to have the verb agree with the object following "of"—in this case, "the people." Since the people are plural, the verb must also be plural ("agree"). Since (a) is correct and (b) is incorrect, both (c) and (d) are incorrect.

37. D: When a phrase is inserted in between the subject and the verb—no matter how long it is—the verb must still agree with the subject, not with the intervening phrase. Therefore, the sentence as written in the question is incorrect because "president" is singular. This error is repeated in (b), with the only change being from "as well as" to "and also." However, (c) is also incorrect because changing the intervening phrase to the conjunction "and" results in two subjects, requiring a *plural* verb for agreement ("are," not "is").

38. B: According to standard English sentence structure, verbs indicating something someone should do (e.g. "recommend," "advise," "require," "suggest," etc.) take the subjunctive of the verb, which is uninflected. Since the concept of "should" is implied by "advise," adding the auxiliary verb "should" (a) is redundant. Another common error is adding *–s* (c) as with other third-person singular nouns, which does not apply here. Putting the verb in past tense (d) is wrong since the sentence describes something to be done ASAP, not something someone did.

39. B: The preposition "to" is NOT used between the verb "let," a subject noun or pronoun, and the verb performed by the subject (e.g. "let me go," "let her try," "let them work," "let him speak," etc.). However, with other verbs with the same/similar meaning, like "allow," "permit," "enable," etc., "to"

IS used and required. Thus (a) incorrectly uses "to" with "let," and (c) incorrectly omits "to" with "allow." "Allow that we take" (d) is also incorrect; "allow us to take" would be correct in standard sentence structure.

40. C: "Lies" is the correct present-tense singular verb. "Lay" (d) is never an intransitive verb; it always takes an object, e.g. "Lay the book on the table." The only way (a) could be correct would be without "that." Still, "...you can see our suburb placed to the east of the city" is awkward; it would read better with "placed" deleted as well. The only way (b) could be correct is to transpose the order of "there is" to "is there," or delete "is."

41. C: This sentence has a subject, verb, adjective, object, and prepositional phrase, all in the correct positions and order, with no errors in person, number, agreement, verb tense, etc. Choice (a) has no verb. Choice (b) has no subject. Choice (d) incorrectly uses the preposition "through" instead of "between," "around," "over," "past," etc. This is a common error, but something/someone solid cannot run *through* toes, or a door. Also, "my" should precede "toes:" I cannot like feeling sand run through anybody else's toes.

42. D: This version is correct. Version (a) has no subject. Version (b) has no auxiliary verb (like "were" or "are" in this example), or a verb like "enjoy," "like," etc., which the progressive participle "watching" requires. Version (c) has the auxiliary verb "are" but incorrectly uses the uninflected/base form of "watch" when it should be the participle "watching" if "are" is used.

43. A: In this complex sentence, the first part provided is the dependent clause. All choices are independent clauses as required, but only (a) fits the meaning. The dependent/subordinate clause's introductory word "Although" signals that the independent clause must express an exception, objection, or contradiction to what the subordinate clause expresses. Choices (b), (c), and (d), however, all state ideas that *agree* with the first part and are thus incorrect.

44. D: This verse is an example of a compound-complex sentence, which has two or more independent clauses one or more dependent clauses. A simple sentence (a) has only one independent clause and no dependent clause. A complex sentence (b) has at least one independent clause and at least one dependent clause. A compound sentence (c) has two or more independent clauses, connected by a coordinating conjunction(s) or semicolon(s). In this example, the first independent clause is "He was chubby and plump;" the second is "I laughed...." The dependent clause is "when I saw him."

45. D: Despite its length or number of words, this is a simple sentence. It is not complex (a) because it has no dependent clause. It is not compound (b) because it has only one independent clause. It is not compound-complex (c) because it does not combine independent and dependent clauses. All of the modifiers, from the beginning through "grocery store," are prepositional phrases modifying verbs or nouns (plus adjectives modifying nouns). The last phrase "and then food shopping" is a verb phrase with a second verb (the first is "going") connected to the same subject ("I").

46. A: This is a compound sentence because it has two independent clauses joined by a coordinating conjunction ("however"). It is not compound-complex (b) or complex (c) because it does not have a dependent clause. It is not a simple sentence (d) because it has more than one independent clause.

47. C: The question is written correctly in the question. When two independent clauses are connected by a conjunctive adverb/adverbial conjunction ("nevertheless" here), it should be preceded by a semicolon and followed by a comma. Choice (a) incorrectly reverses this order. Choice (b) uses two commas instead of a semicolon and comma. Choice (d) replaces the required semicolon before "nevertheless" with a comma and also omits the required comma after "nevertheless."

48. C: This is a complex sentence, with an independent clause ("I got so many things accomplished") and a dependent clause ("while you were sleeping"). Choice (a) is a compound sentence, with two independent clauses (the second is "you were sleeping") joined by a coordinating conjunction ("and"). Choice (b) is a compound-complex sentence, with two independent clauses ("I got things done" and "I took a walk") joined by "and," plus the dependent clause. Choice (d) is a simple sentence, with one independent clause containing two verbs and a prepositional phrase. (It also reads awkwardly).

49. D: This is the correct choice. A compound sentence has two independent clauses connected by a semicolon or conjunction; the latter preceded by a comma. In this case, "so" is the coordinating conjunction. Choices (a) and (c) omit the required comma. Choice (b) incorrectly replaces the comma with a semicolon. For the semicolon to be correct, "so" would not be included.

50. B: This sentence has an independent clause, followed by a dependent clause, followed by a second independent clause—i.e. compound-complex structure—and is correctly punctuated. Version (a) has simple sentence structure, with an adverb phrase instead of a dependent clause and a compound predicate with two verbs instead of two independent clauses. Version (c) has compound structure, i.e. two independent clauses; it lacks a necessary comma between "dressed" and "even," and substitutes a semicolon for a comma before "and." (The semicolon would be *instead* of "and.") Version (d) has simple structure and incorrectly substitutes "going" for "goes."

Mathematics

1. B: The line graph should have a point representing the number of customers at each time, and all the points should be connected by a line. There should be a point at 20 for the time 2:00 p.m., which eliminates every choice except choice B. Double check that the other points are accurate as well. There should be a point at 30 for 4:00 p.m., a point at 50 for the time 6:00 p.m., and a point at 10 for the time 8:00 p.m. Since this is true for all points on the graph for choice B, that is the answer.

2. B: Notice the pattern occurring as the number of minutes increases.

Minute	1	2	3	4
Gallons	28	19	12	7
Change from previous minute		-9	-7	-5

The pattern indicates that in the fifth minute, the number of gallons would decrease by 3.

$$7 - 3 = 4$$

This means 4 gallons of water should be expected to drain.

3. C: There are 3 feet in every yard. Multiply by this conversion factor to find the length in feet.

$$120 \text{ yd} \times \frac{3 \text{ ft}}{1 \text{ yd}} = 360 \text{ ft}$$

Therefore, the length of the football field is 360 feet.

4. B: To convert a mixed number to an improper fraction, multiply the whole number part by the denominator and add the current numerator to get the new numerator of the fraction.

$$3 \times 4 + 3 = 12 + 3 = 15$$

The denominator stays the same. Therefore, the equivalent fraction is $\frac{15}{4}$.

5. A: Use the volume of a rectangular prism formula, $V = l \times w \times h$, to determine the length of the tank. Substitute the known values and solve for l.

$$200 = l \times (8) \times (5)$$
$$200 = 40l$$
$$5 = l$$

Therefore, the length of the tank is 5 feet.

6. C: A diagram of the plot would look like this.

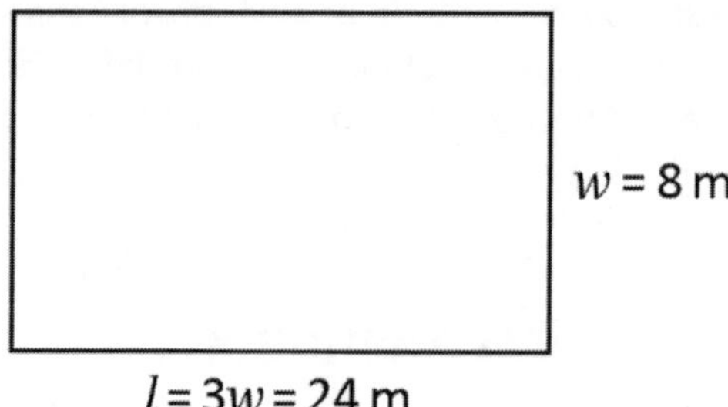

The perimeter of a rectangle can be found using the formula $P = 2l + 2w$. The length is 3 times the width, so the length is 24 meters. Substitute the known values and simplify.

$$P = 2(24) + 2(8)$$
$$P = 48 + 16$$
$$P = 64$$

Therefore, the perimeter of the garden is 64 meters.

7. C: Expressing $\frac{31}{8}$ as the improper fraction $3\frac{7}{8}$ makes this easier to see. It will land between $3\frac{1}{2}$ and 4, which is between points C and D.

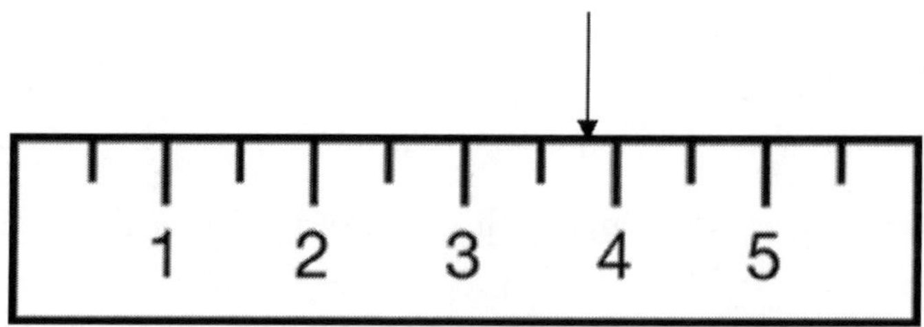

8. C: The pattern in the table is that the number of customers is increasing by 25 each week. This means that there should be $205 + 25 = 230$ customers expected in week 4.

Week	Customers	Change from Previous Week
1	155	
2	180	+25
3	205	+25
4	230	+25

9. C: Use approximation to solve this problem quickly. Mr. Thompson needs about 25 gallons of gas, which costs approximately \$3 per gallon.

$$25 \text{ gal} \times \$3/\text{gal} = \$75$$

Therefore, he needs approximately \$75 to fill his tank. The actual cost to fill the tank is $25.2 \text{ gal} \times \$2.98/\text{gal} = \$75.10$.

10. D: Only choice D correctly shows each amount of salt being subtracted from the original total amount of 26 ounces that was in the box.

11. C: To convert a mixed number to an improper fraction, find the new numerator by multiplying the whole number by the denominator and adding the original numerator.

$$7 \times 8 + 5 = 56 + 5 = 61$$

The denominator stays the same. Therefore, $7\frac{5}{8}$ as an improper fraction is $\frac{61}{8}$.

12. D: Note that the ratio asked for is the number of people who ordered milk to the number who ordered juice. The number of people who ordered coffee does not matter here. This compares 10 to 25, and the order is important here. Since the ratio is with the number of people who ordered milk first, the 10 must come first. So, the ratio is 10 to 25, but the ratio can be written in simpler form by dividing both numbers in the ratio by 5. Therefore, the simplified ratio is 2 to 5.

13. C: To calculate his new hourly rate, add his raise to his original hourly rate.

$$\$15.23 + \$2.34 = \$17.57$$

Therefore, the man's new hourly rate is \$17.57.

14. D: Working the problem backwards, start by adding \$12 to \$17 to find out how much money she had before the movie.

$$\$12 + \$17 = \$29$$

Therefore, Jody had \$29 before she went to the movies. This was half of the money she made at the bake sale.

$$2 \times \$29 = \$58$$

So, Jodi made \$58 at the bake sale.

15. D: First, subtract $5x$ from both sides to get the variable to one side of the equation.

$$2x = 5x - 30$$
$$2x - 5x = 5x - 30 - 5x$$
$$-3x = -30$$

Then, divide both sides by –3 to solve for x.

$$\frac{-3x}{-3} = \frac{-30}{-3}$$
$$x = 10$$

16. A: To solve, test each answer. Notice that in choice A the numerator has been multiplied by 3 to get 12. The denominator has also been multiplied by 3 to get 21. In choice B, the numerator has been multiplied by 4 and the denominator has been multiplied by 5. In choice C, the numerator has been multiplied by 3 and the denominator has been multiplied by 4. In choice D, the numerator has been multiplied by 4 and the denominator has been multiplied by 5. Therefore, choice A is the only correct equation.

17. A: The number of weeks and days can be found by performing long division.

```
     20R5
  7) 145
    -14
      05
    -  0
       5
```

The quotient 20 is the number of weeks, the remainder of 5 is the number of days. Therefore, William will be gone for 20 weeks and 5 days.

18. C: Robinson has the highest number of points. The number of goals and assists need to be added to determine this.

Player	Goals	Assists	Points
Phillips	2	23	$2 + 23 = 25$
Jackson	5	17	$5 + 17 = 22$
Robinson	13	15	$13 + 15 = 28$
Miller	8	19	$8 + 19 = 27$

19. B: A regular pentagon is a 5-sided figure with all sides equal in length. Therefore, the perimeter is $5 \times 6.5 = 32.5$ centimeters.

20. D: Since the marbles are being equally distributed in 4 equal parts, each friend is simply receiving $\frac{1}{4}$ of the marbles. This means he should multiply his number of marbles by $\frac{1}{4}$ and then give that amount to each friend.

21. B: The pattern on the table appears to be an increase of 12 members each year. If there are 43 members in 2010, then $43 + 12 = 55$ members are expected in 2011.

Year	Members	Change from Previous Year
2008	19	
2009	31	+12
2010	43	+12
2011	55	+12

22. A: The simplest way to compare the two pieces of pie is to find a common dominator for both fractions. The older daughter was given $\frac{2}{5}$ of the pie, while the younger daughter was given $\frac{1}{3}$ of the pie. The least common dominator for the two fractions is 15.

$$\frac{2 \times 3}{5 \times 3} = \frac{6}{15}$$
$$\frac{1 \times 5}{3 \times 5} = \frac{5}{15}$$

Therefore, the older daughter received $\frac{6}{15}$ of the pie and the younger daughter received $\frac{5}{15}$ of the pie. $\frac{6}{15}$ is larger than $\frac{5}{15}$, so the older daughter received a larger slice of the pie.

23. C: First, subtract 7 from both sides to isolate x.

$$\frac{x}{3} + 7 = 35$$
$$\frac{x}{3} + 7 - 7 = 35 - 7$$
$$\frac{x}{3} = 28$$

Then, multiply both sides by 3 to solve for x.

$$\frac{x}{3} \times 3 = 28 \times 3$$
$$x = 84$$

24. A: One way to determine which measurement is outside the range is by marking the values on a number line.

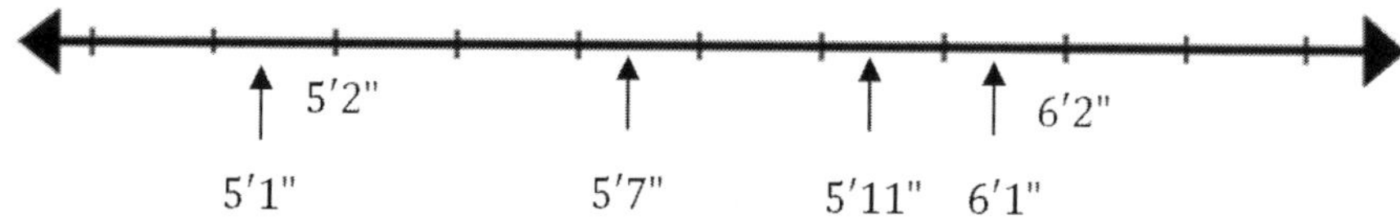

This shows that the height 5'1" is outside the range.

25. C: To simplify this expression, follow the order of operations. First, add what is in the parentheses.

$$20 + 35(4 + 2) + 47$$
$$20 + 35(6) + 47$$

Then, multiply the 6 by 35.

$$20 + 210 + 47$$

Last, we add $20 + 210 + 47$ to get 277.

26. D: The formula for finding the volume of a rectangular prism is $V = l \times w \times h$. Substitute the values given in the question.

$$V = 5 \text{ cm} \times 6 \text{ cm} \times 10 \text{ cm} = 300 \text{ cm}^3$$

The volume of this prism is 300 cm^3.

27. C: The pattern established on the table is that the increase in the number passed is decreasing by 2 each week.

Week	1	2	3	4	5
Number passed	16	25	32	37	40
Change from previous week		+9	+7	+5	+3

Therefore, the students predicted to pass by week 5 will be the value of week 4 plus 3.

$$37 + 3 = 40$$

This means that 40 students are predicted to pass by week 5.

28. C: To find out how much more money Matthew needs, subtract how much he already has from the cost of the game.

$$\$25 - \$18 = \$7$$

Therefore, Matthew needs save \$7 more to purchase the game.

29. D: First multiply the weight of one apple by the number of apples.

$$150 \times 12 = 1{,}800$$

Therefore, a dozen apples weigh 1,800 grams. To convert this value to kilograms, divide by 1,000 because there are 1,000 grams in 1 kilogram.

$$1{,}800 \div 1{,}000 = 1.8$$

Therefore, a dozen apples weigh 1.8 kilograms.

30. C: One way to find this answer is to set up a proportion: $\frac{6}{10} = \frac{G}{240}$, in which G represents the number of Grade 6 students living within two miles of the school. To solve the proportion, cross-multiply.

$$10G = 1{,}440$$

To solve the equation, divide both sides of the equation by 10.

$$G = 144$$

Therefore, Harold should expect 144 students to live within two miles of the school.

31. D: The expression representing the monthly charge for Plan A is $\$20 + \$15(d - 2.5)$, where d is the data used. This can be found by adding the flat rate to the price of any data used over the provided amount. Set this expression equal to the monthly charge for Plan B, which is \$50. Solve for d to find the number of GB for which the two plans charge the same amount.

$$\$20 + \$15(d - 2.5) = \$50$$
$$\$15(d - 2.5) = \$30$$
$$d - 2.5 = 2$$
$$d = 4.5$$

So, the plans have the same cost when Gillian uses 4.5 GB of data.

32. A: Start by finding out how many cans of beans Gerald brought in large boxes by multiplying the number of large boxes by 24.

$$4 \times 24 = 96$$

Therefore, he brought 96 cans in large boxes. Next, find out how many cans of beans he brought in small boxes by multiplying the number of small boxes by 12.

$$6 \times 12 = 72$$

Therefore, he brought 72 cans in small boxes. Finally, add these two numbers together.

$$96 + 72 = 168$$

Gerald brought 168 cans of beans to the food bank.

33. B: It is necessary to find the area of the floor by multiplying the dimensions together. However, since the dimensions are given in feet and we only know the price of carpeting per square yard, converting the dimensions from feet to yards first is helpful. Since there are 3 feet in a yard, dividing each of the dimensions by 3 will give us the measurements in yards.

$$18 \div 3 = 6$$
$$27 \div 3 = 9$$

So, the floor is 6 yards by 9 yards, which is an area of 54 square yards. Last, we multiply 54 by 14, since each square yard costs \$14 and there are 54 square yards.

$$54 \times 14 = 756$$

So, the price of the carpet should be \$756.

34. C: To find the number of days Phil will be gone, start by multiplying 9 by 7 because there are 7 days in a week.

$$9 \times 7 = 63$$

Then, add 5 more days.

$$63 + 5 = 68$$

Therefore, Phil will be gone for 68 days.

35. B: To solve, test each answer. Notice that in choice A, the numerator has been multiplied by 9 to get 18. The denominator has been multiplied by 8. These are not equal fractions. In choice B, both the numerator and denominator have been multiplied by 4. In choice C, the numerator has been multiplied by 4 and the denominator has been multiplied by 2. These are not equal fractions. In choice D, the numerator has been multiplied by 3 and the denominator has been multiplied by 2. These are not equal fractions. Therefore, only choice B is a true statement.

36. A: The ratio asked for is the number of finches compared to the number of sparrows. This compares is the ratio 16 : 20, but the ratio can be written in simpler form by dividing both numbers in the ratio by 4. This gives the ratio 4 : 5. It is important to notice the order of the ratio. Since the number of finches is written before the number of sparrows, the ratio must be 16 to 20 and not 20 to 16. Also, note that the number of wrens or jays does not matter here.

37. D: The recipe is being multiplied by 4 in this problem.

$$\frac{1\text{ cup of milk}}{8\text{ cupcakes}} = \frac{4\text{ cups of milk}}{32\text{ cupcakes}}$$

So, a total of 4 cups of milk are needed. Since this is not one of the choices, a conversion is needed.

$$1\text{ pint} = 2\text{ cups}$$
$$1\text{ quart} = 2\text{ pints}$$

Therefore 1 quart = 4 cups, meaning Mary needs 1 quart of milk.

38. B: There are 36 out of 100 yellow cars in the sample. Since the parking lot has $\frac{1}{4}$ as many cars as the sample, $\frac{1}{4}$ as many yellow cars should be expected.

$$36 \times \frac{1}{4} = 9$$

Therefore, 9 yellow cars are expected to be in the lot.

39. C: The approximate price of the fence is found by rounding to 70 feet at $4 per foot.

$$\text{Price} = 70\text{ ft} \times \$4/\text{ft} = \$280$$

Therefore, he will spend approximately $280 on fencing. The actual price is 71 ft × $3.98/ft = $282.58.

40. A: Use the area formula for a square: $A = s^2$. Substitute the known information into the equation and solve for s.

$$81 = s^2$$
$$s = \pm 9$$

Since the side of the garden is a length, it must be positive. Therefore, the length of one side of the garden is 9 feet.

41. A: The distance from the top of the tire to the ground that is given is the diameter of the tire. The distance around the tire is the circumference. To find the circumference, multiply the diameter, 20, by π. Since 3 is fairly close to the value of π, multiplying by 3 will give a good estimate of the distance around each tire.

$$3 \times 20 = 60$$

Therefore, the distance around each tire is approximately 60 inches.

42. B: Since the two lines are parallel, it follows that the angles δ and θ are equal. The angles α and θ are supplementary angles. That is, they add up to 180°. It follows that:

$$\theta = 180° - \alpha = 180° - 135° = 45°$$

Since $\delta = \theta$, then $\delta = 45°$.

43. D: Each month should have a point at the value given at the table, and all the values should be connected with a line. February should have a point at 2, which eliminates choice A. June should have a point at 8, which eliminates choice B. August should have a point at 5, which eliminates choice C. Choice D has these 3 points and a point for October at 10, which means it is the correct line graph.

44. D: Add a 3rd column to represent improvement. This would be the second score minus the first score for each of the students.

Student	First Score (words per minute)	Second Score (words per minute)	Improvement
Alexander	22	39	$39 - 22 = 17$
Betty	39	48	$48 - 39 = 9$
Carolyn	27	43	$43 - 27 = 16$
David	22	42	$42 - 22 = 20$

David has the greatest improvement of 20 words per minute between the two tests.

45. C: A straight angle is 180°. Subtract 45° from 180° to find the measure of $\angle AEB$.

$$180° - 45° = 135°$$

Therefore, $m\angle AEB = 135°$.

Practice Test #2

Verbal

1. To look for information in a library, users should know that call numbers are for what?

A. Shelving items by their subjects
B. Shelving items by page count
C. Shelving items by author name
D. For (a) and (c), but not for (b)

2. Which of the following library resource access points was enabled by the digital revolution?

A. Title
B. Subject
C. Keyword
D. Author name

3. If you are in a public library, which of these classification systems would you most expect to find being used for storing and locating information sources?

A. The Dewey Decimal Classification system
B. The Library of Congress Classification system
C. The National Library of Medicine Classification
D. Public libraries typically use any or all these

4. If you had to research a subject and were given a book list or bibliography and/or had conducted an internet search, in which order should you do these to evaluate a book's usefulness for your topic?

A. Look at the subject index; scan the table of contents; read the title, and subtitle if any.
B. Read the title, and subtitle if any; scan the table of contents; look at the subject index.
C. Scan the table of contents; read the title, and subtitle if any; look at the subject index.
D. Look at the subject index; read the title, and subtitle if any; scan the table of contents.

5. Following directions that tell how to do something requires which of these skills?

A. Understanding language regardless of interest in the activity
B. Attention, comprehension, interest in activity, and motivation
C. Motivation to follow directions, irrespective of comprehension
D. Interest in the activity, whether attending to directions or not

6. Which of the following represents a common hierarchy of types/levels of directions?

A. Basic one-step, expanded one-step, basic two-step, expanded two-step, and complex
B. One-step directions, two-step directions, three-step directions, and complex directions
C. Basic directions, one-step directions, two-step directions, and more complex directions
D. One-step, two-step, expanded two-step, three-step, expanded three-step directions

7. Suppose you are given four pictures involving cookies and some other objects, accompanied by this statement: "Circle the letter of the picture of cookies that are not on a plate and are next to the milk." Which of the following must you notice and understand to choose the correct picture?

A. The use of negatives only
B. The meanings of prepositions
C. The use of both negatives and positives
D. Preposition meanings, negatives, and positives

8. Of the following, which is the best reason for thoroughly reading all directions in a series before starting to follow them?

A. It is just a good principle in general to read everything thoroughly first.
B. You might not understand the first directions without reading the last.
C. The last direction(s) might tell you to follow only some of earlier ones.
D. You might find it easier to follow some later steps before earlier ones.

9. In *Julius Caesar,* William Shakespeare wrote the well-known line of dialogue, "This was the most unkindest cut of all." This solecism intentionally uses which instance of incorrect grammar?

A. A double superlative
B. A dangling participle
C. Abnormal syntax
D. A split infinitive

10. When conducting electronic searches for information in libraries, using which Boolean operator will make the search broader?

A. AND
B. OR
C. NOT
D. ( )

11. When we read literature and other written information, which type of connection do we make when we can relate something in the text to something we already knew or experienced personally?

A. Text to self
B. Text to text
C. Text to world
D. None of these

12. Of the following, which work of literature is narrated in the third person?

A. "The Tell-Tale Heart" by Edgar Allan Poe
B. *Great Expectations* by Charles Dickens
C. *Little Women* by Louisa May Alcott
D. *Robinson Crusoe* by Daniel Defoe

13. "Will you be ______ the dinner?"

A. attend
B. attends
C. attended
D. attending

14. In the following sentence, what change would make the meaning clearer? "Advertised for sale was a table by a lady with hand-carved legs."

A. Move "for sale" to follow "a table."
B. Move "by a lady" to follow "for sale."
C. Move "was a table" before "for sale."
D. The meaning is clear with no change.

15. In which of these sentences is the underlined word correct in context?

A. "The theme is of man <u>verses</u> nature."
B. "This poem has a great many <u>verses</u>."
C. "This poem is written in free <u>verses</u>."
D. "This marriage is for better or <u>verse.</u>"

16. Which of these means to reduce, as in intensity?

A. Abate
B. Abjure
C. Abdicate
D. Abrogate

17. "You will be assigned to a group of employees with <u>commensurate</u> experience." What is the best definition of the underlined word?

A. Complementary
B. Superior
C. Inferior
D. Equal

18. "I admire his <u>probity</u> as a person." What does the underlined word mean?

A. Depth
B. Strength
C. Honesty
D. Curiosity

19. There are still some ______houses standing in the Atlanta, Georgia, area. Which word has a suitable meaning?

A. Antediluvian
B. Antiquarian
C. Antebellum
D. Antecedent

20. Three of these words are synonyms and one is an antonym of the others. Which one is the antonym?

A. Encomium
B. Accolade
C. Eulogy
D. Obloquy

21. Among these multiple meanings of the word *bark*, which one is figurative?

A. Our dog will never bark at the mailman.
B. His bark is certainly worse than his bite.
C. The birch trees have light-colored bark.
D. I always bark my shins on that ottoman.

22. In which of the following sentences does the meaning of the underlined word have the part of speech of an adverb?

A. I saw the bird light on a branch.
B. You are travelling awfully light.
C. Her light skin is easily sunburnt.
D. The light of the sun was bright.

23. The missing words in each sentence sound the same but have different meanings. In which sentence is the missing word also spelled differently than the others?

A. They say a woman's work is never_____.
B. One horse is black; the others are _____.
C. He pays bills timely, yet they ______ him.
D. A mayfly or shadfly is also called a _____.

24. Among multiple meanings of the word *skate,* which of these is NOT included?

A. A boot with a blade(s) or wheels
B. To slide or roll with smoothness
C. These are all included meanings
D. A ray-like fish of North America

25. Many critics have accused the current Congress of a feckless lack of action. What can readers unfamiliar with the underlined word identify as its *best* meaning(s) in this sentence?

A. Irresponsible or indifferent
B. Ineffective or incompetent
C. Rash, careless, or heedless
D. (a) and/or (b) instead of (c)

26. The meaning of *ambidextrous* can be informed by words sharing the same Latin prefix in common. Which is/are NOT included among these?

A. Ambivalent
B. Ambulance
C. Ambiguous
D. All of these

27. Which of these sentences provides a context to determine the meaning of the underlined word for those unfamiliar with it?

A. Bob and Carol were impecunious, but Ted and Alice were not.
B. Skydiving is not a sport recommended for impecunious people.
C. That community offers many services for impecunious citizens.
D. The impecunious couple could not afford to feed their children.

28. In which of the following sentences is the underlined word used correctly?

A. The baleful glare of the villain frightened the children.
B. The farmer stored many a baleful of hay for his horse.
C. The crew had to baleful buckets from the leaking boat.
D. She was known for her baleful and helping disposition.

29. Of the following, which one is a complete sentence?

A. We wait.
B. Waiting for hours.
C. Waited for a very long time.
D. Since we have been waiting for so long.

30. Which of these is an example of a sentence fragment rather than a complete sentence?

A. She cried.
B. Birds fly.
C. We take.
D. He ate.

31. Of the following versions, which has (a) correct and complete sentence(s) throughout?

A. Until we meet again.
B. Until we meet again, I will think of you.
C. Until we meet again. I will think of you.
D. Until we meet again, which will be soon.

32. Among these choices, where is a sentence that is complete grammatically?

A. Underneath the bed.
B. I found him hiding underneath.
C. Hiding underneath the bed.
D. I found him hiding underneath the bed.

33. "Our love and understanding of this country is built upon this belief." Which is the correct version of this sentence?

A. Our love and understanding of this country is built on this belief.
B. Our love and understanding of this country is built on these beliefs.
C. Our love and understanding of this country are built upon this belief.
D. Our love and understanding of this country are building to that belief.

34. "The bunch of beautiful wildflowers brighten up the desk." What is correct?

A. brightens up
B. brighten up
C. brightened up
D. brightening up

35. If there is one pie, which sentence is correct?

A. A lot of the pies are gone.
B. A lot of the pie are gone.
C. A lot of the pies is gone.
D. A lot of the pie is gone.

36. Which of these is correctly written?

A. There's a lot of people in that building.
B. There are a lot of people in that building.
C. There is a lot of people in that building.
D. Theirs a lot of people in that building.

37. Of the following different sentences, which one uses the right grammar?

A. Seven miles are too long to walk home.
B. Ten years are the maximum sentence.
C. A hundred dollars seem a lot to spend.
D. A hundred dollar bills were in the box.

38. "_______ was caused by a contaminated water supply." Which choice follows standard sentence structure to complete this?

A. The pandemic's starting
B. The outbreak of the pandemic
C. How the pandemic got started
D. That the pandemic it started

39. "I would have been glad to join you if only I _______ the time." Filling the blank with which of the following would give this sentence standard structure?

A. would have had
B. have had
C. had had
D. had

40. "We are really _______ our cousins next month." To complete this with standard syntax, which choice is correct?

A. looking forward to visiting
B. anticipating to visiting
C. wish to visit
D. hoping visit

41. Which of these versions uses correct sentence structure?

A. On the beach, two people who are enjoying the fine weather.
B. On the beach, two people who enjoy the fine weather.
C. On the beach, two people are enjoying the fine weather.
D. On the beach, two people enjoying the fine weather.

42. "I did receive your message yesterday, and I will send you a reply by tomorrow." What kind of sentence is this?

A. Simple
B. Complex
C. Compound
D. Compound-complex

43. "I saw him last week when we both attended the meeting, but we did not speak." Which of the following identifies the structure of this sentence?

A. It is a compound-complex sentence.
B. It is a compound sentence.
C. It is a complex sentence.
D. It is a simple sentence.

44. "Go look upstairs in the laundry hamper inside the cabinet under the shelf in the larger of the two bathrooms for those pants and that shirt." What structure does this sentence have?

A. Compound-complex
B. Compound
C. Complex
D. Simple

45. "I saw them at the beach. They were playing volleyball." Which choice converts these two sentences into one compound sentence?

A. I saw them at the beach playing volleyball.
B. I saw them at the beach; they were playing volleyball.
C. I saw them at the beach, while they were playing volleyball.
D. I saw them at the beach, where they were playing volleyball.

46. "I want to go to the movie, ________." What choice will complete this to have compound-complex sentence structure?

A. but my mother wants me to finish my homework first.
B. but my mother will not let me until I finish my homework.
C. which would be a lot more fun than doing this homework.
D. instead of staying here and having to do all this homework.

47. "They found the first visit so enjoyable, but they plan to go back again." What will correct the error in this sentence AND still maintain its compound sentence structure?

A. They found the first visit so enjoyable that they plan to go back again.
B. They found the first visit enjoyable; however, they plan to visit again.
C. They found the first visit so enjoyable, and they plan to go back again.
D. They found the first visit so enjoyable and are planning to visit again.

48. Which choice is a complex sentence without any errors?

A. Even though he started first, he finished last.
B. Even though he started first; he finished last.
C. Even though he started first he finished last.
D. Even though he started first. He finished last.

49. Of the following, which has no errors and compound-complex sentence structure?

A. I heard sounds while walking down the hall and saw people in one of the rooms.
B. I heard sounds, as I walked down the hall; and I saw people in one of the rooms.
C. Walking down the hall, I heard sounds, I saw several people in one of the rooms.
D. I heard sounds as I walked down the hall, and I saw people in one of the rooms.

50. Which version of this sentence is correct?

A. Owen Wilson's nose is crooked and bumpy, as if it has been broken, yet his face is appealing.
B. Owen Wilson's nose is crooked and bumpy; as if it has been broken; yet his face is appealing.
C. Owen Wilson's nose is crooked and bumpy as if it has been broken; yet, his face is appealing.
D. Owen Wilson's nose is crooked and bumpy, as if it has been broken yet his face is appealing.

Mathematics

1. If $\frac{x}{3} + 27 = 30$, what is the value of x?

A. 3
B. 6
C. 9
D. 12

2. One cold afternoon at a small café, 20 people drank hot tea, 45 drank coffee, and 15 drank hot chocolate. Which ratio compares the number of people who drank coffee to the number who drank tea?

A. 4 to 13
B. 4 to 9
C. 9 to 4
D. 3 to 1

3. If a cube's side length is 5 cm, what is the volume of the cube?

A. 15 cm^3
B. 65 cm^3
C. 105 cm^3
D. 125 cm^3

4. A girl scores a 99 on her math test. On her second test, her score drops by 15. On the third test, she scores 5 points higher than she did on her second. What was the girl's score on the third test?

A. 79
B. 84
C. 89
D. 99

Refer to the following for question 5:

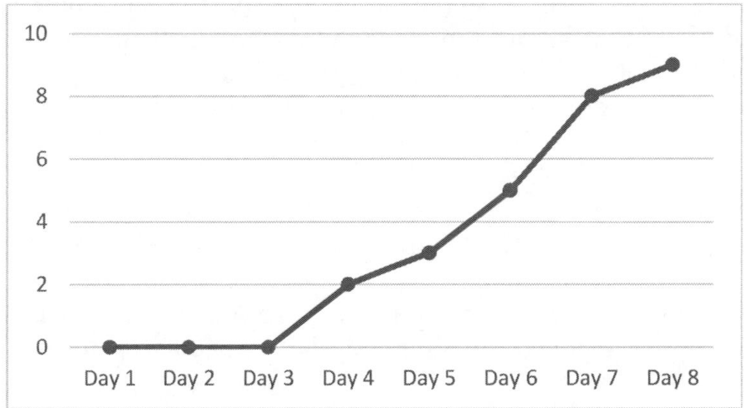

Beth plants a number of sunflower seeds and checks daily to see if any have sprouted. The graph above shows how many seedlings are growing each day when she checks.

5. Which day did the first seedling appear?

A. Day 1
B. Day 2
C. Day 3
D. Day 4

6. A woman weighs 145 pounds. She gains 12 pounds one month and 6 pounds the next month. What is her new weight?

A. 148 pounds
B. 151 pounds
C. 157 pounds
D. 163 pounds

7. A man goes to a casino with $125. He loses $30 on blackjack, then he loses another $40 on roulette. How much money does he have left?

A. $35
B. $40
C. $55
D. $70

8. A woman has 60 ornaments. She decides to divide them evenly among her 3 grandchildren. How many ornaments will each child receive?

A. 10
B. 15
C. 20
D. 30

9. If a number, x, is subtracted from 27, the result is –5. What is the value of x?

A. 22
B. 25
C. 32
D. 35

10. If $3a + 5b = 98$ and $a = 11$, what is the value of $a + b$?

A. 13
B. 24
C. 33
D. 65

11. It rained every day last week except Friday. If it rained twice as much on Monday as it did on Thursday, which of the following graphs could model the week's rainfall in inches?

A.

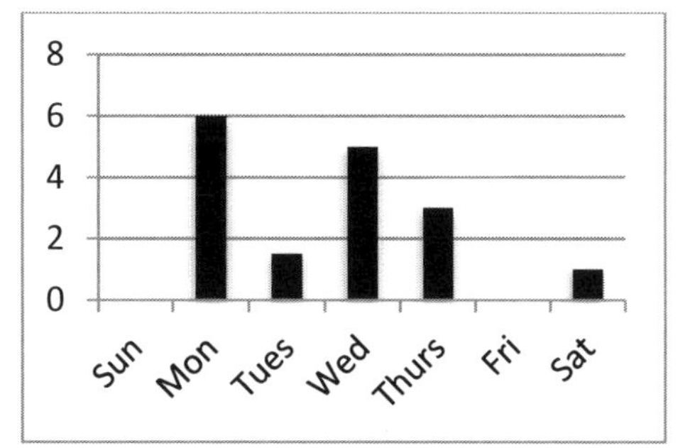

C.

8
6
4
2
0
Sun
Mon
Tues
Wed
Thurs
Fri
Sat

B.

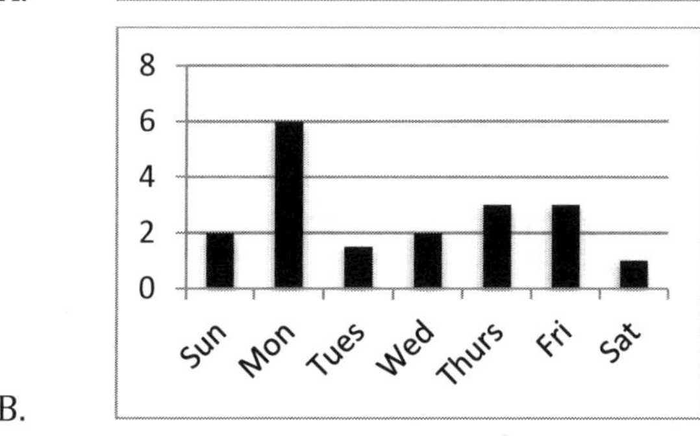

D.

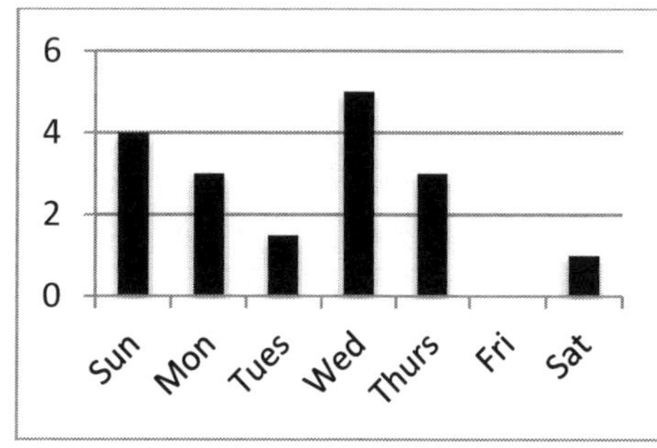

12. A senior citizen was billed $3.85 for a long-distance phone call. The first 10 minutes cost $3.50, and 35 cents was charged for each additional minute. How long was the telephone call?

A. 20 minutes
B. 17 minutes
C. 15 minutes
D. 11 minutes

13. A grocery manager sells 2 bags of potatoes for each bag of carrots. He also sells 6 bags of onions for each bag of potatoes. If he sells 12 bags of onions, how many bags of carrots will he sell?

A. 1
B. 2
C. 3
D. 4

14. At the middle school Vanessa attends, there are 240 Grade 6 students, 210 Grade 7 students, and 200 Grade 8 students. Which ratio best compares the number of students in Grade 8 to the number of students in Grade 6 at Vanessa's school?

A. 5 : 6
B. 5 : 11
C. 6 : 5

D. 7 : 8

15. A 24-foot-tall building casts a shadow that is 6 feet in length. If a dog next to the building casts a shadow 0.75 feet long, how tall is the dog?

A. 1.5 feet
B. 2 feet
C. 2.5 feet
D. 3 feet

16. What is the area of a rectangle with sides 34 meters and 12 meters?

A. 408 m^2
B. 40.8 m^2
C. 22 m^2
D. 2.83 m^2

17. A dress is marked as 20% off. With the discount, the current price is $40.00. What is the price of the dress without the discount?

A. $32
B. $45
C. $48
D. $50

18. A woman buys 23 pounds of potatoes. She gives 10% of them to a neighbor and 15% of them to her mother. How many pounds does she have left?

A. 20.70 pounds
B. 19.55 pounds
C. 17.25 pounds
D. 12.63 pounds

19. A couple plans to buy a dining room table. They have $569 in a joint bank account. The man has $293 in additional cash and the woman has $189. What is the most expensive table they will be able to afford?

A. $482
B. $758
C. $862
D. $1,051

20. Carlos helped in the library by putting new books on the shelves. Each shelf held between 21 and 24 books. Each bookcase had 5 shelves and Carlos filled 2 of the bookcases. Which number is nearest to the number of books Carlos put on the shelves?

A. 100
B. 195
C. 215
D. 245

21. A woman must drive 298 miles to reach her destination. If she travels 42 miles during the first day, how many miles will she have left to travel?

A. 225
B. 256
C. 271
D. 286

22. Which of these would best illustrate the percentage of a budget allocated to various departments?

A. Pie chart
B. Line graph
C. Box-and-whisker plot
D. Venn diagram

23. An armoire was purchased for $340.32 at an auction, subject to a 5% tax rate. What was the additional tax charged on the armoire?

A. $15.82
B. $16.02
C. $16.39
D. $17.02

24. If one plant requires 2 liters of water each day, how many liters are required to water the plant for 13 days?

A. 6.5 liters
B. 15 liters
C. 26 liters
D. 39 liters

25. Petra installed 10 light fixtures at a new warehouse that was being built. Each of the fixtures required 3 light bulbs. The bulbs come in packages of 5 and cost $8 per package. What was the total cost for the bulbs required for all the fixtures Petra installed at the warehouse?

A. $16
B. $48
C. $120
D. $240

26. A farmer has 360 cows. He decides to sell 45. Shortly after, he purchases 85 more cows. How many cows does he have?

A. 230
B. 315
C. 400
D. 490

27. The two prisms shown below are similar. What is the measurement of x?

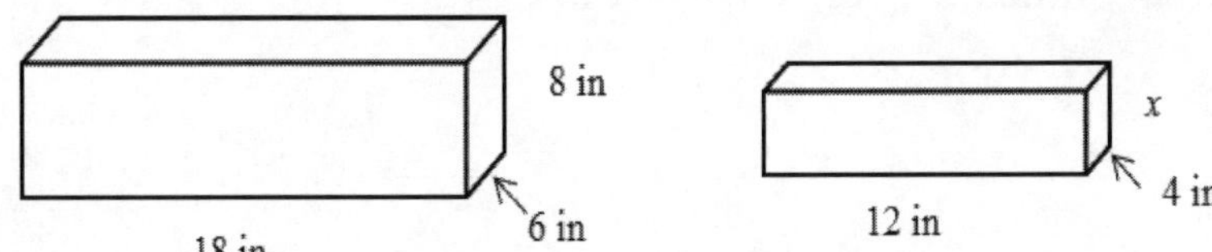

A. $4\frac{3}{4}$ in
B. $5\frac{1}{3}$ in
C. $5\frac{2}{3}$ in
D. $5\frac{3}{4}$ in

28. Annette read that out of 20 televisions sold in her state last year, 3 were Brand V. If a furniture store near her home sold 360 televisions last year, about how many should Annette expect to be Brand V?

A. 18
B. 54
C. 1,080
D. 2,400

29. A duck pond has 350 ducks. If 75 go south for the winter, how many ducks will still be in the pond?

A. 250
B. 275
C. 300
D. 325

30. 9.5% of the people in a town voted for a certain proposition in a municipal election. If the town's population is 51,623, about how many people in the town voted for the proposition?

A. 3,000
B. 5,000
C. 7,000
D. 10,000

31. A triangle has a base measuring 12 cm and a height of 12 cm. What is its area?

A. 24 cm^2
B. 56 cm^2
C. 72 cm^2
D. 144 cm^2

Refer to the following for question 32:

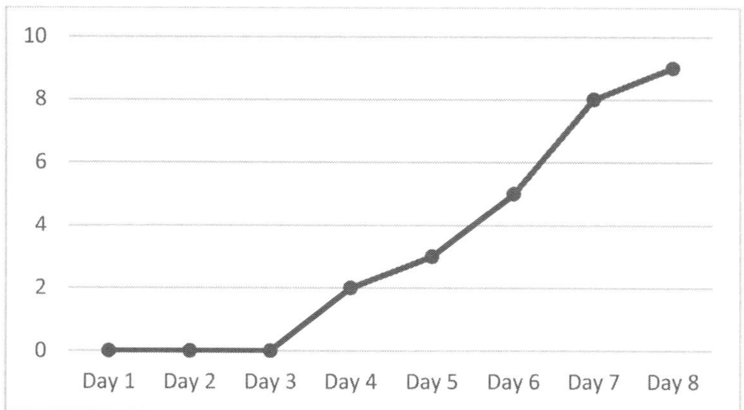

Beth plants a number of sunflower seeds and checks daily to see if any have sprouted. The graph above shows how many seedlings are growing each day when she checks.

32. How many seeds sprouted on Day 8?

A. 0
B. 1
C. 4
D. 9

33. If $3x - 30 = 45 - 2x$, what is the value of x?

A. 5
B. 10
C. 15
D. 20

34. Antoinette had $50 to spend on fun things for herself. At a craft show, she bought 2 pairs of earrings for $10 each and a picture for $12. She also spent $7 on lunch. If she spent no other money, how much money should Antoinette have left from the $50?

A. $35
B. $25
C. $21
D. $11

35. A rectangular solid measures 12 cm by 3 cm by 9 cm. What is its volume?

A. 36 cm^3
B. 108 cm^3
C. 324 cm^3
D. 407 cm^3

36. Janet makes homemade dolls. Currently, she produces 23 dolls per month. If she increased her production by 18%, how many dolls would Janet produce each month? Round to the nearest whole number.

A. 27
B. 32
C. 38
D. 40

37. If one van can carry 6 people, how many vans are needed to carry 250 people?

A. 40
B. 41
C. 42
D. 43

38. A rectangular garden has a perimeter of 600 yards. If the length of the garden is 250 yards, what is the garden's width in yards?

A. 25 yards
B. 50 yards
C. 175 yards
D. 350 yards

39. If 24 people tried to climb a mountain and 6 people completed the climb, what percentage of people did NOT complete the climb up the mountain?

A. 25%
B. 30%
C. 75%
D. 80%

40. If $a = 3$ and $b = 4$, simplify the following expression: $6a + b - 7$

A. 12
B. 15
C. 20
D. 22

41. Five workers each earn $135/day. What is the total amount earned by the five workers for one day of work?

A. $675
B. $700
C. $725
D. $750

42. A skyscraper is 548 meters high. The building's owners decide to increase its height by 3%. How high would the skyscraper be after the increase? Round to the nearest whole number.

A. 551 meters
B. 555 meters
C. 562 meters
D. 564 meters

43. Evan measured the amount of rain in the gauge over the weekend. On Saturday, he measured $1\frac{6}{10}$ inches and on Sunday, $\frac{8}{10}$ inches. What is the total amount of rain, in inches, Evan measured on those two days, written in the simplest form?

A. $1\frac{14}{20}$
B. $1\frac{3}{10}$
C. $1\frac{2}{5}$
D. $2\frac{2}{5}$

44. If one dog eats 5 pounds of food each week, how many dogs will 65 pounds of food feed for a week?

A. 11
B. 12
C. 13
D. 14

45. Candace's shoelace broke. She measured the unbroken shoelace and finds that she needs a replacement lace that is at least 16 inches long. The store has the following lengths available.

$$15\frac{7}{10}, 16.25, \frac{47}{3}, 15.5$$

Which one of the following lace lengths would be long enough to replace the broken shoelace?

A. 15.5
B. $15\frac{7}{10}$
C. $\frac{47}{3}$
D. 16.25

Answer Key and Explanations for Test #2

Verbal

1. D: In libraries, call numbers are used to classify items for shelving them according to subject (a). The second part of the call number usually identifies the author's name (c); however, they are not sorted by page count (b).

2. C: The title (a) of a book, periodical, or other item in a library; the subject (b) of the item; and the name of the author (d) are all access points that have been available to users historically. However, accessing resources by keyword (c) is an innovation accompanying digital materials. Without knowing an item's title, its author's name, or even looking in only certain subject areas, users can enter keywords to search specifically across all these other access points.

3. A: The Dewey Decimal Classification (DDC) system is the one most often used by the majority of public libraries in the United States. The Library of Congress (LC) Classification system (b) is the one most often used by the majority of university, college, and research libraries in the US. The National Library of Medicine (NLM) Classification is the system most often used by health science collections and libraries in colleges and universities. Therefore, (d) is incorrect.

4. B: To evaluate whether or not or how much a book will be useful for your research, first read the book's title, and the subtitle if there is one. Then scan the table of contents to see whether or how much the chapter titles and topics apply to your research subject. Then look at the subject index in the back of the book to see how many words or terms it includes that are key to your topic focus, and how many pages of the book address these terms or topics.

5. B: Following directions that tell the reader how to do something requires paying attention to the directions, understanding the language used in the directions, being interested in the activity to which the directions apply, and motivation to follow the directions. Comprehension without interest (a), motivation to follow directions without comprehending them (c), and interest in the activity without paying attention to the directions (d) are all insufficient for following directions correctly.

6. A: A common hierarchy that ranks direction types in order of their levels from simplest to most complex is basic one-step directions (e.g. "Close the door"); expanded one-step directions, which add negatives and/or contractions and slightly more advanced vocabulary (e.g. "Show me the one that isn't yellow"); two-step directions (e.g. "Close the door and then sit down"); expanded two-step directions, which add a structure to two steps (e.g. "Clean up your desk before you come to the meeting"); and complex directions, which include later-developing vocabulary and syntax and complex sentence structure (e.g. "Please silence all digital devices after having gone to your stations.").

7. D: The sample direction quoted in the question requires the reader to notice and understand preposition meanings "on" and "next to", the use of a negative "<u>not</u> on a plate", and the use of a positive "<u>are</u> next to the milk," rather than only the use of a negative (a), only the meanings of prepositions (b), or the use of negatives and positives (c) but not prepositions, in order to follow all parts of this instruction correctly.

8. C: A common error many adults make with directions is following one step at a time without reading all steps first. Sometimes later steps direct NOT following earlier ones. A quiz (www.eslmania.com) highlights this error by giving directions in 10 steps; step #10 says, "Follow only steps #1 and #2." Those not reading all steps in advance follow steps #3 through #9, making #10 impossible. Hence the best reason is not simply on general principle (a); because later steps explain earlier ones (b), or because following them out of order is easier (d): well-written directions are sequenced correctly.

9. A: This uses a double superlative ("most" + "unkindest"). A dangling participle (b) is "Walking down the street, the house was on fire"—a phrase containing a verb participle, within a sentence omitting the associated subject. This is rarely if ever used intentionally in literature for confounding, not emphasizing meaning. Unusual syntax (c) Shakespeare used in *Twelfth Night* is: "....no woman...Shall mistress be of it...." A split infinitive (d) is "to really succeed." While commonplace today, it is seldom used intentionally in literature as many correct alternatives usually exist.

10. B: AND (a) *narrows* a search by specifying both/all terms it connects; the search will not return documents containing only one/some of those terms. OR (b) *broadens* a search by specifying either, both, or all terms entered. NOT (c) *narrows* a search by specifying no records containing terms following it. Parentheses (d) *narrow* a search, customizing it to a particular topic, by searching parenthetical terms first. For example, searching "(tobacco or smoking) and cancer" returns documents including tobacco and cancer, smoking and cancer; and tobacco, smoking, and cancer; but *not* documents including smoking and tobacco *without* cancer.

11. A: Text-to-self connection involves relating text to one's own prior knowledge and/or experience. Text-to-text (b) connection involves relating one text to something similar (or different/opposite) in another text/other texts, i.e. text synthesis. Text-to-world (c) connection involves relating something in the text to real life, though not necessarily the reader's personal experience. For example, a reader might make a text-to-world connection between a book about war and an actual war. Connecting text to a real-life war the reader also personally experienced, e.g. as a soldier, involves both text-to-self and text-to-world connections. Thus (d) is incorrect.

12. C: In *Little Women,* Alcott narrates the novel in the third person; i.e. she describes the characters using names and pronouns "she," "her," "he," "him," "they," "them," etc. as if she were observing them from outside of the story. In (a), Poe uses the first-person narrative voice with pronouns "I," "me," "my," etc., writing as the main character speaking directly to the audience to tell his tale. In (b), Dickens tells the story in the first person from the viewpoint of Pip, the protagonist. In (d), Defoe also relates the tale in first person from the main character's perspective.

13. D: The context gives the auxiliary verb "will" indicating the future tense, and the linking verb "be" indicating the progressive participle; hence the correct form is "attending." "Attend" (a) would be correct if the sentence did NOT contain "be", e.g. "Will you attend the dinner?" "Attends" (b) is always incorrect with "you;" the *–s* ending indicates third-person singular, e.g. "S/he attends the dinner." "Attended" (c) indicates the past tense, e.g. "You attended the dinner last night."

14. B: The sentence as written in the question has a misplaced modifier: the lady did not have hand-carved legs; the table did. The change to "Advertised for sale by a lady...." Choice (b) would correct this and clarify meaning; so would "Advertised by a lady for sale...." Choice (a) would not correct the error. Choice (c) would also leave the misplaced modifier unchanged. Therefore, (d) is incorrect.

15. B: "Verses" is the plural of "verse," i.e. a line in a poem or song. Choice (a) incorrectly uses "verses" instead of "vers**us**," derived from Latin, meaning "against," and often abbreviated as "vs." People who make this all-too-common error are not only ignorant of the correct spellings and meanings of these two words; they likely also mispronounce "versus" by voicing the final *s* to sound like /z/ as in "verses" instead of like /s/ as in "versus." The term for unrhymed, unmetered poetry is free *verse*, NOT "verses" (c). The expression is "for better or *worse,"* NOT *"verse"* (d).

16. A: To abate means to reduce in intensity, e.g., Wait until the rain—or the publicity, or the furor—abates. To abjure (b) means to recant, retract, take back; repudiate, renounce, forswear, or give up under oath; or to shun or avoid. To abdicate (c) means to relinquish, give up, or renounce, especially formally, as a throne, position, office, power, authority, right, responsibility, or claim. To abrogate (d) means to abolish, repeal, revoke, or annul, as a law or contract; or to put an end to or put aside something.

17. D: Commensurate means equal, corresponding, proportionate, or having a common measure. Complementary (a) means completing or perfecting something (e.g. their skills are not the same as yours but complement them). Superior (b) means better than; inferior (c) means worse than.

18. C: Probity means honesty, integrity, and uprightness. It derives from Latin *probāre* meaning to prove, which in turn is derived from Latin *probus* meaning good or worthy. Although it ultimately shares a common root with *probe*, it does not mean depth (a) or curiosity (d). It does not mean strength (b) either.

19. C: Antebellum means before the war, and particularly the American Civil War. Antediluvian (a) means before the flood, i.e. during Biblical times, specifically the times described in the Old Testament book of Genesis before the flood for which Noah built an ark. Antiquarian (b) means related to ancient times or the study of antiquities, or interested/dealing in old or rare books. Antecedent (d) simply means before, prior, or preceding; or a preceding thing, event, phenomenon, circumstance; or, in plural, ancestors, or details of earlier life.

20. D: Encomium (a) means a formal expression of high praise. Accolade (b) is a synonym meaning laudatory praise or an honor or award. Eulogy (c), another synonym, can mean formal high praise of someone who has died, or simply high praise or commendation. Obloquy (d) is an antonym of these words, meaning censure, criticism, aspersion, calumny, or the resulting disgrace or ill repute.

21. B: The word *bark* has multiple meanings. The meanings of dog vocalization (a), the outer surface of a tree (c), and injuring by bumping into something (d) are all literal meanings. However, the common expression in (b), though it uses terms (bark and bite) associated with a dog, typically refers figuratively to a human, meaning someone's words/voice sound/threaten worse than his/her actions. "His bark is worse than his bite" means what he says/the way he says it (like yelling, which *bar*k also represents figuratively) is worse than what he does.

22. B: In sentence (a), *light* is a verb meaning to land or settle. In (b), it is an adverb modifying the verb and indicating how, meaning with little baggage. In (c), it is an adjective modifying the noun, describing it as light, meaning pale in color. In (d), it is a noun meaning illumination or radiance.

23. A: The missing word in (a) is *done,* the perfect (present perfect, past perfect, or future perfect) of the verb *to do.* It is pronounced the same but spelled *dun* in (b), (c), and (d). In (b), it is an adjective referring to a tan or grayish-brown color. In (c), it is a verb meaning to demand payment persistently and insistently. In (d), it is a noun *meaning* a mayfly or shadfly (another synonym).

24. C: These are all included among multiple meanings of the word *skate*. It can be a noun meaning a boot with a blade(s) or wheels (a); a verb meaning to slide, glide, or roll smoothly (b) across ice, water, the ground, or a floor; or a fish of the Rajidae family, resembling rays, and found along the Pacific coast of North America.

25. A: Given the choices here, readers unfamiliar with the meaning of *feckless* can identify the correct meaning from a clue in the sentence context: this adjective modifies "lack of action." If the accusation is that Congress does not take action, the meaning must be (a). If the accusation were of feckless *action*, then the meaning would be (b): action *was* taken but was ineffective or incompetent. Meaning (c) defines the word *reckless* rather than *feckless.* Since only (a) is correct, (d) is incorrect.

26. B: The Latin-derived prefix *ambi-* means both or on both sides. In *ambidextrous,* it means using both hands equally well. It is also in *ambivalent* (a), meaning having divided feelings or unable to choose between two sides; and *ambiguous* (c), meaning open to more than one interpretation, unclear, or equivocal. However, *ambulance* (b), meaning a medical transport vehicle, has a different Latin-derived prefix, *ambul-*, meaning to walk (*ambulate* and *ambulatory* share this prefix). Since only (b) is correct, (d) is incorrect.

27. D: Sentence (a) does not provide context clues to the word's meaning. From syntax it is an adjective but could mean anything describing people. Sentence (b) gives a little more information, but still the word could mean many things: skydiving is not recommended for people who cannot stand, walk, jump; fear heights, flying; are risk-averse, overweight, prone to fractures, etc. Similarly, in (c), it could mean disabled, illiterate, lonely, sociable, friendly, active, athletic, curious, newly arrived, etc. Only (d) informs meaning through context: Since they could not afford to feed their children, impecunious means impoverished.

28. A: Baleful means evil, malign, menacing, or harmful; the sentence context helps to inform this definition by using the words "villain," "glare," and "frightened." While (b) and (c) might sound right in speech, the only correct ways to write them are as separate words "bale full" in (b) and "bail full" in (c). In (d), the word is incorrectly used to mean its opposite: helping is an antonym for baleful.

29. A: Although this is the shortest choice, it is a complete sentence with a subject, "We," and a verb, "wait." Choice (b) is not a complete sentence because it has no subject. Choice (c) is not a complete sentence for the same reason: though longer, it has a verb and modifying prepositional phrase, but no subject. Choice (d) has a subject (we) and verb (have been waiting), but the subordinating conjunction "since" makes it a dependent clause, which must accompany an independent clause. Eliminating "while" makes it an independent clause and a complete sentence.

30. C: Choice (a) has a subject (She) and intransitive verb (cried) which does not need an object, and expresses a complete idea; thus, it is a complete sentence. The same is true of (b) and (d). However, (c) has the transitive verb "take," which needs an object in this context, and does not express a complete thought; so, it is not a complete sentence. Adding an object, e.g. "We take walks," would complete it.

31. B: This version opens with a dependent clause and finishes with an independent clause following the comma. Version (a) has only the dependent clause with no independent clause to complete it and thus is not a sentence. Version (c) separates the two clauses into individual sentences incorrectly because the first clause is dependent and not a sentence. Version (d) begins with the dependent clause and continues with another dependent, relative clause modifying it, but still has no independent clause and hence is not a sentence.

32. D: This choice is a grammatically complete sentence. It has a subject, verb, direct object, and prepositional phrase modifying the verb. Choice (a) has only the prepositional phrase with no subject or verb. Choice (b) has a subject, verb, direct object, and a preposition that should introduce a prepositional phrase but does not—underneath what? Choice (c) finishes the prepositional phrase with "the bed" and has a verb, but is missing the subject.

33. C: The sentence has two subjects (love and understanding), so the verb should be plural ("are"), not singular ("is") as in (a) and (b). (Version (b) also changes the meaning by making the object "belief" plural.) Version (d) changes the meaning by changing "are built upon this" to "are building to that."

34. A: The verb must be singular ("brightens") to agree with the singular subject ("bunch"). The sentence as written in the question and choice (b) incorrectly uses the plural ("brighten") as if the plural object ("wildflowers") were the subject. Choice (c) changes the meaning by putting the verb in the past tense ("brightened") instead of the present tense. Choice (d) uses the progressive participle ("brightening"), which is ungrammatical and would require an auxiliary verb like "is" ("is brightening").

35. D: With the phrase "a lot of"—like "some of," "most of," "all/all of," "the majority of," "the minority of," and others indicating portions—the verb must agree with the noun following "of." In this case, (d) is correct. While (a) is also grammatically correct, the question specifies ONE pie, and both the object "pies" and verb "are" are plural. Since "pie" is correctly singular in (b), the verb "are" is incorrectly plural. The reverse is true in (c): "pies" is incorrectly plural AND the verb "is" singular, causing subject-verb disagreement.

36. B: In this sentence, the subject is "people," not "there." Hence, to agree with the plural subject, the verb must also be plural, i.e. "are." The singular "is" is incorrect, whether spelled out (c) or contracted (a). While a singular verb is incorrect here, even in another sentence requiring a singular verb, the contraction of "there is" is "there's," not "theirs" (d), which is the third-person plural possessive pronoun (e.g. "That house is theirs"), so (d) is doubly wrong.

37. D: This sentence is the only correct one because dollar bills are individual pieces, so a hundred of them would be plural ("were"). However, seven miles IS too long to walk home (a); ten years IS the maximum sentence (b); and a hundred dollars SEEMS a lot to spend (c), because in each case the subject is treated as a unit—multiple miles but one distance (a), multiple years but one time period (b), and multiple dollars but one money amount (c)—and a singular subject takes a singular verb.

38. B: Choice (a) is nonstandard and even reads awkwardly: "starting" is not normally a subject noun (although "beginning" is). "Outbreak" plus the prepositional phrase "of the" (b) instead of apostrophe-*s* are more appropriate. Combining "how [it] got started" and "was caused by" (c) is redundant, as is combining noun and pronoun ("the pandemic" and "it") for one subject as in (d). However, even without "it," "that the pandemic started" is not a good subject with "was caused by." This construction is more suited to, for example, "That the pandemic started is not open to debate."

39. C: This conditional-subjunctive construction uses the subjunctive (would) and conditional (if) in the past perfect tense (had had). Conditional is one tense behind subjunctive.* While "would have" is correct in the subjunctive, it is NEVER correct in the conditional (a). Choice (b) is present perfect, not past perfect; it would never accompany a past conditional-subjunctive. Simple past tense (d) is a common conditional error in conditional-subjunctive constructions. *It would only be correct with a present-tense subjunctive, e.g. "I would join you if I had the time." (*Future-present: "I will join you if I have the time.")

40. A: "Visiting" maintains parallel form with "looking (forward to)." However, while we look forward TO something, we do NOT anticipate "to" something; we anticipate it (b). The auxiliary verb "are" signals that it helps a main verb in the progressive (-ing) participle; hence "wish" (c) is incorrect. Either "We are really wishing" OR "We really wish" without "are" would be correct. "Hoping" is the correct participle; but like it lacks the necessary "to" (as with "looking forward") before "visit."

41. C: The progressive ("-ing") participle of a verb requires an auxiliary verb like "are," "is," "was," "were," "has/have been," "had been," "will be," "to be," etc. Version (a) adds the relative pronoun "who," making "two people...." a dependent clause. With no independent clause, this is not a sentence. The same is true of (b). Version (d) omits the auxiliary verb, making "enjoying the fine weather" into a verb phrase modifying the subject "people," which then lacks an actual verb.

42. C: This is a compound sentence, i.e. it has two independent clauses joined by a coordinating conjunction ("and"). (They could also be joined by a semicolon instead of a conjunction.) Either one of these clauses by itself (and without "and") would be a simple sentence (a). A complex (b) sentence has at least one independent clause and at least one dependent clause. A compound-complex sentence (d) has at least two independent clauses and at least one dependent clause.

43. A: This is a compound-complex sentence. The two independent clauses are "I saw him last week" and "we did not speak." The dependent clause is "when we both attended the meeting." The coordinating conjunction connecting the two independent clauses is "but." It is not a compound sentence (b) because it has a dependent clause. It is not a complex (c) sentence because it has two independent clauses rather than one.

44. D: Simple sentences are not necessarily short/few in words; this is an example. The subject is called "you understood" (i.e. the sentence is addressing "you" as the subject without actually naming "you," but this is understood by the reader). The verb is "Go look," a serial verb. All modifiers are prepositional phrases, not clauses. The sentence has no dependent clause to make it complex (c) and only one independent clause, not two as in compound (b) sentences. Compound-complex (a) sentences have two or more independent clauses and one or more dependent clauses.

45. B: A compound sentence has two independent clauses joined by a semicolon, as they are here, or a coordinating conjunction. Choice (a) is not a compound sentence but a simple sentence; the gerund phrase (verb phrase) "playing volleyball" modifies the object pronoun "them." Choice (c) is a complex sentence: "while they were playing volleyball" is a dependent/subordinate clause. Choice (d) is also a complex sentence, with the dependent clause "where they were playing volleyball."

46. B: Adding (a) to the independent clause in the question creates a compound sentence, i.e. one with two independent clauses but no dependent clause. A compound-complex structure is created by (b), which adds not only another independent clause (but my mother will not let me) but also a dependent clause (until I finish my homework). A complex sentence is produced by (c), which adds a dependent clause without another independent clause. Adding (d) makes it a simple sentence, with "to go" modified by a prepositional phrase with two verb phrases.

47. C: The error in the sentence is the word "but." Planning to go back/visit again does not conflict with enjoying the first visit. Replacing "but" with "and" (c) as coordinating conjunction corrects this while maintaining compound sentence structure, i.e. two independent clauses. Version (a) corrects the error, but makes the structure complex by introducing the second clause with subordinating conjunction "that," making it a subordinate/dependent clause. Version (b) reproduces the original error, substituting "; however," for ", but." Version (d) makes the structure simple, with two verbs ("found" and "are planning").

48. A: This is a complex sentence, with the dependent clause before the comma and the independent clause after the comma. Version (b) incorrectly uses a semicolon instead of a comma. A semicolon is used between two independent clauses in a compound sentence, not between dependent and independent clauses in a complex sentence. Version (c) incorrectly omits punctuation between clauses. Version (d) is two simple sentences rather than one complex sentence.

49. D: This compound-complex sentence has an independent clause, a dependent clause, and another independent clause, connected by a comma and conjunction. Choice (a), with only one independent clause and no dependent clause, is a simple sentence with a modifying adverb phrase ("while walking down the hall") and a compound predicate, with verbs "heard" and "saw." Choice (b) is punctuated incorrectly: the comma should be omitted, and the semicolon should be a comma. Choice (c) has no dependent clause and incorrectly substitutes a comma for a semicolon between "sounds" and "I saw."

50. A: This is a compound-complex sentence, correctly punctuated with commas between the first independent clause, the dependent clause, and the second independent clause. Version (b) incorrectly places a semicolon between clauses: A semicolon connects independent clauses *instead of* a comma and conjunction, and does NOT connect independent and dependent clauses. Version (c) omits the comma between the first independent clause and the dependent clause, substitutes a semicolon for the comma after the dependent clause, and incorrectly places a comma after the conjunction "yet." Version (d) omits the necessary comma before the dependent and second independent clause.

Mathematics

1. C: First, subtract 27 from both sides of the equation to isolate x.

$$\frac{x}{3} + 27 = 30$$

$$\frac{x}{3} + 27 - 27 = 30 - 27$$

$$\frac{x}{3} = 3$$

Next, multiply both sides by 3.

$$\frac{x}{3} \times 3 = 3 \times 3$$

$$x = 9$$

2. C: The ratio compares the number of coffee drinkers to the number of tea drinkers, in that order, so the ratio is 45 to 20. Note that the ratio of 20 to 45 would be incorrect. The ratio of 45 to 20 can then be written in simpler terms by dividing both terms by 5 to get 9 to 4. Notice that the number of hot chocolate drinkers is not important in this problem.

3. D: Because it is a cube, we can find the volume by taking the cube of the side length.

$$5 \times 5 \times 5 = 125$$

Therefore, the volume of the cube is 125 cm^3.

4. C: First, calculate her score on the second test.

$$99 - 15 = 84$$

Then, calculate her score on the third test.

$$84 + 5 = 89$$

Therefore, she made an 89 on the third test.

5. D: For Days 1, 2, and 3 (choices A, B, and C) on the chart, the number of seedlings is 0. Day 4 is the first time we see the line move away from 0, showing that 2 seedlings sprouted that day.

6. D: To calculate her new weight, add her weight increases (12 pounds and 6 pounds) to her original weight (145 pounds).

$$145 + 12 + 6 = 163$$

Her new weight is 163 pounds.

7. C: Start by calculating how much money the man lost.

$$\$40 + \$30 = \$70$$

Then, subtract that amount from the amount he had originally.

$$\$125 - \$70 = \$55$$

The man has $55 left.

8. C: To calculate how many ornaments each grandchild will receive, divide the total number of ornaments by the number of people they will be divided between.

$$60 \div 3 = 20$$

Each grandchild will receive 20 ornaments.

9. C: To solve this problem, first write it as an equation: $27 - x = -5$. From here, solve using normal algebra methods.

$$\begin{aligned} 27 - x &= -5 \\ -x &= -32 \\ x &= 32 \end{aligned}$$

10. B: First solve for b. If $3a + 5b = 98$ and $a = 11$, then the equation below can be solved.

$$\begin{aligned} 3(11) + 5b &= 98 \\ 33 + 5b &= 98 \\ 5b &= 65 \\ b &= 13 \end{aligned}$$

Therefore, $a + b = 11 + 13 = 24$.

11. C: We are looking for a graph with two key pieces of information: rainfall every day except Friday, and an amount of rain on Monday double the rain on Thursday. Answer choice A is incorrect because it shows no rain on Sunday. Answer choice B is incorrect because it shows rain on Friday. Answer choice D is incorrect because the amount of rain on Monday is equal to the amount of rain on Thursday. Only answer choice C is correct because it shows no rain on Friday, 6 inches on Monday, and 3 inches on Thursday.

12. D: If the first 10 minutes of the call cost \$3.50 and the total charge was \$3.85, subtract \$3.50 from \$3.85 to get \$0.35. Each additional minute cost \$0.35. So, the call was 10 minutes plus 1 additional minute, for a total of 11 minutes.

13. A: First, figure out how many bags of potatoes would be sold if 12 bags of onions were sold. The ratio of onions sold to potatoes sold is $6 : 1$. So, if he sells 12 bags of onions, we must divide this number by 6 to get the number of bags of potatoes sold.

$$12 \div 6 = 2$$

He sold 2 bags of potatoes. Then, use this number to figure out how many bags of carrots he would sell. The problem tells us that he sells 2 bags of potatoes for each bag of carrots. Therefore, he would sell 1 bag of carrots if he sold 12 bags of onions.

14. A: One way to answer this question is to name the ratio: $200 : 240$. Then, write the ratio in simplest terms by dividing both terms by the greatest common factor, 40, to get $5 : 6$. It should be noted that the number of Grade 7 students is not important for this problem. Also, the order of the ratio matters. Since it asks for the ratio using the number of Grade 8 students first, the ratio is $200 : 240$ and not the other way around.

15. D: The following proportion may be written and solved for x: $\frac{24}{6} = \frac{x}{0.75}$. Use cross multiplication to solve for x.

$$24 \times 0.75 = 6x$$
$$18 = 6x$$
$$3 = x$$

Thus, the dog is 3 feet tall.

16. A: To find the area of a rectangle, multiply the length by the width.

$$34 \text{ m} \times 12 \text{ m} = 408 \text{ m}^2$$

Therefore, the area of the rectangle is 408 m^2.

17. D: If the dress's price is 20% off, it is $(100\% - 20\%) = 80\%$ of the regular price. So, the sales price of the dress, \$40, is 80% of what price? To find the answer, divide 40 by 80%, which is equivalent to the fraction $\frac{80}{100}$. Dividing by the fraction $\frac{80}{100}$ is the same as multiplying by its reciprocal, $\frac{100}{80}$. $40 \times \frac{100}{80} = 40 \times \frac{5}{4} = \frac{200}{4} = 50$, so, the original price was \$50.00.

18. C: First, calculate 10% of 23 pounds.

$$23 \times 0.10 = 2.3$$

Then, calculate 15% of 23 pounds.

$$23 \times 0.15 = 3.45$$

These two values can be added to calculate the total number of pounds given away.

$$2.3 + 3.45 = 5.75$$

The woman gave away 5.75 pounds of potatoes. Finally, subtract this value from the original total to calculate how many pounds she has left.

$$23 - 5.75 = 17.25$$

She has 17.25 pounds of potatoes left.

19. D: Calculate the total amount of money the couple has available to spend, which is the amount in the joint bank account and the amount that each person has.

$$\$569 + \$293 + \$189 = \$1{,}051$$

The couple can afford a table that costs up to $1,051.

20. C: First, since there are 5 shelves on each of the 2 bookcases, we multiply 5 by 2 to get 10 shelves total. Then, we find the minimum and maximum number of books that could have filled the shelves. Since $21 \times 10 = 210$ and $24 \times 10 = 240$, the number of books he shelved must be between 210 and 240.

21. B: To calculate how many miles the woman still has to travel, subtract the distance she has traveled (42 miles) from the distance she originally had to travel (298 miles).

$$298 - 42 = 256$$

She has 256 miles left to travel.

22. A: A pie chart shows the relationship of parts to a whole. A line graph is often used to show change over time. A box-and-whisker plot displays how numeric data are distributed throughout the range. A Venn diagram shows the relationships among sets. Therefore, a pie chart would best illustrate the percentage of a budget allocated to various departments.

23. D: To determine the tax, you must calculate 5% of $340.32. Note that 5% = 0.05. So, you multiply 340.32 by 0.05.

$$\begin{array}{r} 340.32 \\ \times\ 0.05 \\ \hline 17.0160 \end{array}$$

Since you want cents here, the digit 6 rounds up the 1 left of it to a 2, which results in 17.02. Therefore, the additional tax charged on the armoire was $17.02.

24. C: To calculate this value, multiply the number of liters the plant needs each day by the number of days it must be watered.

$$2 \times 13 = 26$$

Therefore, 26 liters are required to water the plant for 13 days.

25. B: To answer this question, find the total number of bulbs required by multiplying 10 by 3.

$$10 \times 3 = 30$$

The number of packages of bulbs required can be found by dividing this total number of bulbs, 30, by 5.

$$30 \div 5 = 6$$

This means that 6 packages were needed. Then, multiply 6 by the cost per package, 8, to find the total cost of purchasing bulbs for the warehouse.

$$6 \times 8 = 48$$

Therefore, Petra spent $48 on light bulbs for the warehouse.

26. C: First, calculate how many cows he has after selling 45.

$$360 - 45 = 315$$

Then, calculate how many cows he has after buying 85 more.

$$315 + 85 = 400$$

The farmer now has 400 cows.

27. B: Since the figures are similar, the following proportion may be written and solved for x.

$$\frac{6}{4} = \frac{8}{x}$$
$$6x = 4 \times 8$$
$$6x = 32$$
$$x = \frac{32}{6} = 5\frac{2}{6} = 5\frac{1}{3}$$

Therefore, the measure of x is $5\frac{1}{3}$ in.

28. B: One method that can be used to answer this question is to write and solve the proportion $\frac{3}{20} = \frac{V}{360}$, where V stands for the number of Brand V televisions that were sold at the furniture store. To solve the proportion, we can cross multiply.

$$20V = 1{,}080$$

We solve this equation by dividing both sides of the equation by 20.

$$V = 54$$

Therefore, she should expect 54 of the televisions sold to be Brand V.

29. B: To calculate the number of ducks left, subtract the number of ducks that left from the number of ducks that were originally there.

$$350 - 75 = 275$$

There are 275 ducks left in the pond.

30. B: The number of people who voted for the proposition is 9.5% of 51,623. If we only require an approximation, we can round 9.5% to 10%, and 51,623 to 50,000. Then 9.5% of 51,623 is about 10% of 50,000, or $0.1 \times 50{,}000 = 5{,}000$. Therefore, about 5,000 people voted for the proposition.

31. C: The area of a triangle can be calculated by using the following formula.

$$A = \frac{1}{2}bh$$

Substitute the values given in the question into the equation.

$$A = \frac{1}{2}(12)(12) = 72$$

Therefore, the area of the triangle is 72 cm^2.

32. B: The graph shows the number of seedlings that are growing at any given time. On Day 8, 9 seedlings were growing (though this is answer choice D, be careful not to stop here). On Day 7, 8 seedlings were growing, so 1 seed sprouted on Day 8.

33. C: First, move all the variable terms to one side and the constants to the other side, and combine like terms.

$$3x - 30 = 45 - 2x$$
$$3x + 2x = 45 + 30$$
$$5x = 75$$

Then, divide both sides by 5 to solve for x.

$$\frac{5x}{5} = \frac{75}{5}$$
$$x = 15$$

34. D: Antoinette bought 2 pairs of earrings at $10 each. To find the amount of money spent on the earrings, 10 must be multiplied by 2. Then adding that $20 to the $12 she paid for the picture and adding $7 for lunch, she spent $39 in all.

$$\$50 - \$39 = \$11$$

Therefore, Antoinette should have $11 left after her shopping spree.

35. C: The formula for finding the volume of a rectangular solid is $V = \text{length} \times \text{width} \times \text{height}$.

$$\begin{aligned} V &= l \times w \times h \\ &= (12\text{ cm}) \times (3\text{ cm}) \times (9\text{ cm}) \\ &= 324\text{ cm}^3 \end{aligned}$$

Therefore, the volume of the rectangular solid is 324 cm^3.

36. A: First, calculate 18% of 23.

$$0.18 \times 23 = 4.14$$

Then, add this value (the increase) to the original value of 23.

$$23 + 4.14 = 27.14$$

Rounding to the nearest whole number, we get 27. Therefore, she would produce 27 dolls each month.

37. C: To calculate the number of vans needed, divide the total number of people that must be transported by the number of people each van can carry.

$$250 \div 6 \approx 41.66$$

Since this value is more than 41, it must be rounded up to 42 because 41 vans will not have enough room to carry all the people.

38. B: The equation for perimeter of a rectangle is $P = 2l + 2w$. Substitute the perimeter and the length and solve for the width.

$$\begin{aligned} 600 &= 2(250) + 2w \\ 600 &= 500 + 2w \\ 100 &= 2w \\ 50 &= w \end{aligned}$$

Therefore, the width of the garden is 50 yards.

39. C: Of the 24 people that set out to climb, only 6 made it to the top so 18 people did not complete the climb because $24 - 6 = 18$. This means that $\frac{18}{24}$, which can be simplified to $\frac{3}{4}$ by dividing both the numerator and denominator by 6, of the people did not complete the climb. The fraction $\frac{3}{4}$ is equivalent to the percentage 75%. So, 75% of the people did not complete the climb up the mountain.

40. B: To simplify this expression, start by substituting in the given values.

$$6(3) + (4) - 7$$

From here, use the order of operations to simplify.

$$18 + 4 - 7 = 22 - 7 = 15$$

41. A: Each earns \$135, so to find the total earned, that amount must be multiplied by the number of workers.

$$135 \times 5 = 675$$

Therefore, the total amount earned by the five workers for one day of work is \$675.

42. D: First, calculate 3% of 548 meters.

$$0.03 \times 548 \text{ m} = 16.44 \text{ m}$$

Add this increase to the building's original height.

$$548 \text{ m} + 16.44 \text{ m} = 564.44 \text{ m}$$

Rounding to the nearest whole number, we get 564 meters. Therefore, the new height of the skyscraper will be 564 m.

43. D: To answer this question, note that the fractions have common denominators. When adding fractions with common denominators, we need to add only the numerators, so, the sum of $\frac{6}{10}$ and $\frac{8}{10}$ is $\frac{14}{10}$. This should then be written as a mixed number, $1\frac{4}{10}$, which is found by dividing 14 by 10 which gives the whole number and the remainder becomes your new numerator over the same denominator of 10. The fraction $\frac{4}{10}$ can also be written as $\frac{2}{5}$ by dividing numerator and denominator by the common factor of 2. Therefore, $\frac{14}{10}$ is equivalent to $1\frac{2}{5}$. Be careful here to remember the 1 from the original $1\frac{6}{10}$ amount given in the problem, which must be added to the $1\frac{2}{5}$ to make a total of $2\frac{2}{5}$.

44. C: To calculate this value, divide the total amount of food by the amount of food each dog requires.

$$65 \div 5 = 13$$

Therefore, 65 pounds of food will feed 13 dogs for a week.

45. D: It is easier to think as the required 16 inches as 16.00 and convert all answer choices to a decimal to compare. Anything greater than 16.00 would be sufficient. $15\frac{7}{10}$ is equal to 15.7, $\frac{47}{3}$ is equivalent to 15.67, and 15.5 remains 15.5. These three choices are all slightly less than the required 16.00 inches; therefore making 16.25 inches the only adequate choice.

It's Your Moment, Let's Celebrate It!

Share your story @mometrixtestpreparation